Self-Regulated Learning

Practical Interventions for Struggling Teens

Norman Brier

Research Press   2612 North Mattis Avenue, Champaign, Illinois 61822
(800) 519-2707   www.researchpress.com

Composition by Jeff Helgesen
Cover design by Linda Brown, Positive I.D. Graphic Design, Inc.
Printed by Seaway Printing, Inc.

ISBN-13: 978–0–87822–631–3
Library of Congress Control Number 2010925156

To Nelia

*Whose memory inspires effort, persistence, and kindness
in working towards valued goals*

Contents

Figures

Introduction

For over 35 years, I have directed an adolescent division at the Albert Einstein College of Medicine in Bronx, New York, which serves youth with multiple emotional and behavioral issues, often including a history of chronic school failure. During this time, it has become apparent that intervention attempts that focus exclusively on the remediation of academic skills for this population are insufficient to produce meaningful gains in academic achievement. The feelings of hopelessness and helplessness that these youth have come to experience and expect in regard to their ability to learn interferes with their desire to approach academic tasks, seek help, and exert effort.

To help these students achieve better outcomes, I developed two programs focused on academic motivation. The first, *Enhancing Academic Motivation: An Intervention Program for Young Adolescents* (Brier, 2006), provides a series of structured lessons designed primarily for classroom use. The second, *Motivating Children and Adolescents for Academic Success: A Parent Involvement Program* (Brier, 2007), offers parents the information they need to influence their children's academic motivation in a positive way.

Rationale and Purpose

While these programs have helped students become more willing to attempt learning tasks and to sustain these attempts, it is apparent that, often, many of these youth still lack self-discipline. In particular, a sizable portion of youth seem to have difficulty in planning, apportioning, and scheduling their time and effort to achieve a goal; in monitoring their progress; and in adjusting their strategies and behavior when necessary. Interventions focused narrowly on teaching study or organizational skills are not enough for many students, especially those with a history of chronic school failure.

Exercising the skills involved in self-regulation—self-awareness, attention management, self-evaluation, and so forth—is critical in determining academic success or failure. The interventions in this book, appropriate for

1

students in upper elementary school through high school, address specific difficulties in self-regulation and can be used along with other interventions designed to facilitate academic skills and motivation. The first part of each chapter presents a summary of the literature pertinent to the component of academic self-regulation covered in the chapter. The second part presents a number of interventions based on this empirical literature.

Specifically, interventions are designed to help youth increase their academic self-regulation by enhancing their ability to do the following:

► Exercise willpower and make the choice to increase their efforts to act in a self-regulated manner when performing academic tasks

► Develop detailed academic goals to increase feelings of academic mastery

► Employ a future time perspective that includes positive intentions and images of how they might be or ought to be

► Form positive expectations about academic success and competence

► Identify values and interests that facilitate school engagement

► Create strategies to achieve academic goals, including strategies for seeking help

► Manage attention and resist distractions, in part by using private speech

► Develop an academic self-concept and a "possible self" that increases hope, self-discipline, and feelings of self-efficacy

► Experience positive emotions and mood and manage distressing emotions, including urges to act in a perfectionistic or procrastinating manner

► Elicit contextual support from parents, teachers, and peers

Using the Materials in This Book

The interventions can be carried out in either the clinical or educational setting. Mental health professionals as well as counselors, social workers, and psychologists in schools can use the literature reviews and techniques provided in a comprehensive effort to help youth referred for problems with academic self-regulation. Interventions may also be used selectively to address specific needs. Although the interventions are written with reference to a one-to-one approach, the material is readily adaptable for small-group and classroom use, with chapters forming the basis for sessions to help students enhance their level of academic self-regulation.

Figures throughout the book—questionnaires, checklists, and so on—may be photocopied from the book or printed from the accompanying CD. Vignettes illustrating the experiences of learners with a variety of self-regulation issues also appear throughout the text. Intended to capture attention and illustrate specific points, these stories and related follow-up questions are provided in reproducible form on the CD to give you the option of providing a printed copy.

Preintervention and Postintervention Assessment

The Academic Self-Regulation Checklist (ASC), provided in Appendix A and on the CD, is a screening tool used as part of the intervention. By administering the checklist during the initial session and again in the final session and then comparing the results, you can use it to evaluate the effectiveness of the interventions you use. The ASC can also be used as a diagnostic tool during the first session to gain information about a youth's particular strengths and weaknesses in regard to academic self-regulation, and at the end of the intervention to determine the nature of any additional help needed. Scoring instructions are provided in the appendix.

A Final Word

In this book, I have attempted to provide a sound knowledge base with regard to the multiple factors that influence academic self-regulation and, based on these empirical findings, to help practitioners by creating a set of tools that they can use to enhance youngsters' self-control while engaging in learning tasks. It is my sincere hope that using these tools to address self-regulation issues directly will help youth achieve better academic outcomes.

1

Components of Academic Self-Regulation

OVERVIEW

For many students, school becomes an increasingly negative experience as they advance in grade. As a result, they often have difficulty seeing academic tasks as relevant, interesting, and engaging and lack the self-discipline necessary to succeed in school. They feel disengaged and do not demonstrate a high level of effort, set academic goals, consider strategies to accomplish tasks, or monitor their performance and progress. In addition, disengaged students are less likely to take responsibility for the consequences of their academic choices; they avoid exerting and maintaining willpower, especially if doing so is experienced as unpleasant, and they have difficulty managing attention (Hidi & Harackiewicz, 2000).

Students who exhibit these negative characteristics are said to have problems with *academic self-regulation*—that is, they have problems exerting self-control and maintaining self-discipline when engaging in school tasks (Zimmerman, 2008). In contrast, students with academically self-regulated attitudes and behaviors can study or perform a challenging or repetitive school task, even when there is something else that they enjoy doing more (Blair, 2002).

Students who are academically self-regulated can carry out three particular academic tasks especially well:

► Setting academic goals and relevant performance standards

► Creating strategies to attain goals and maintain the performance standards they have set

5

► Monitoring their actions to make sure they are acting consistently with their goals and performance standards and adjusting their academic behavior based on this information (Bandura, 1997; Carver & Scheier, 1982; Hoeksma, Oosterlaan, & Schipper, 2004)

The three essential components of academic self-regulation—planning, problem solving, and self-evaluation—usually occur in a specific sequence (Cleary & Zimmerman, 2002; Zimmerman, 2008).

Planning

Academically self-regulated students take time to plan. They think about their academic goals and consider whether the goals are relevant, valuable, interesting, and achievable. Once they set a goal, these students are motivated to achieve the goal and act autonomously to do so. They exert effort, feel confident, and expect to succeed. They are also engaged while learning and persist at tasks until they are completed (Bandura, 1997; Urdan & Midgely, 2001). Academically self-regulated youth view the goal as a target or destination, can use the goal to prioritize tasks, and can decide where to direct their attention. They know how to use time frames to schedule and pace their academic activities (Bandura & Cervone, 1986).

Problem Solving

Students who are academically self-regulated understand and use problem-solving strategies. They select strategies to achieve their goals, sequence the strategies selected, set standards to gauge the quality of their performance, manage their attention, and monitor the degree to which they are acting in accordance with their standards and making progress in achieving their goals. If they become frustrated along the way, these students work to overcome the problem. They do not procrastinate and are aware of discrepancies among their actions, goals, and performance standards. When discrepancies are noted, academically self-regulated learners use this information to adjust their efforts and strategies. In addition, they try to take advantage of the help available and use routines and structure to help get their work done.

Self-Evaluation

Academically self-regulated learners engage in self-evaluation. They compare the results of their efforts with their intentions, attach meaning to the outcome, and think about whether they have acted according to their own standards or principles. When pleased with the results, these youth experience positive emotions that further enhance their academic motivation. When they are not happy with the results, they often become distressed but, when they do, they can use that feeling as motivation to improve.

INTERVENTIONS

1.1 Assessment of Academic Self-Regulation Skills

Tell the student that you want her to be a "scientist" and to collect "data" about how she actually does in setting academic goals, selecting strategies, and monitoring her schoolwork. Provide a copy of and review the **Academic Self-Regulation Checklist** (in Appendix A and on the CD) and ask the student to indicate how often she had the thought or took the action described in the checklist, based on her actions and attitudes during the past month of school.

1.2 Comparison and Self-Assessment

To help a student become more aware of his own attributes pertaining to academic self-regulation and have a set of words to facilitate self-description in this regard, present the following two vignettes. The first describes a teenager with poor academic self-regulation skills; the second is about a teen with well-developed skills. Depending on the student's level of intellectual and academic competence, you can read the vignettes aloud or ask the student to read them to himself.

Vignette A: Sam

Sam is 15. He is very bright and yet very bored by school. He loves robotics. He sees school as irrelevant to his interests. Sam's only academic goal is to get through the school day as quickly and painlessly as possible. He doesn't take pride in how he does at school, although he gets upset when other students, who he feels are not as smart as he is, get on the honor roll when he does not.

Although Sam finishes most of his schoolwork, he does not check it to be sure that he followed the instructions or did the work accurately. Similarly, he does not pay careful attention when he writes down his homework assignments, nor does he plan a time to do the work. He usually does his homework at the last minute and often hands it in either incomplete or with errors.

Sam's mother tells him over and over that he has to care more about school, that it is important, and that he should try harder. She doesn't ask him how he would like to do things differently, and she criticizes him for not "owning up" to his bad study habits and for not trying to do some of the things his teacher suggests that he do to improve. Frustrated, she sent Sam to an after-school program where, again, the teacher told Sam what he needs to do to "improve." When Sam mentions his interest in robotics to the after-school teacher and asks to do something with robotics as part of the program, the teacher says that he is too far behind with his regular work and that all his time has to be spent on catching up. Sam doesn't feel interested in the material the teacher presents and, just like in his regular classes, he tunes the teacher out.

Vignette B: Suzanne

Suzanne is 12. She is a serious student who wants to do the right thing at school all the time. In class, she keeps her desk so neat and organized that the teacher uses it as an example of how other children should keep their desks.

Suzanne has strong values. She has the goal of doing her work well but hates feeling competitive. She is critical of students who brag about being on the honor roll, especially to other students who are not on it. She tries to keep track of her progress and not get discouraged when she "messes up." Instead, she sits down with her parents and tries to strategize and think about what she could do differently. Once she has a plan, Suzanne tries to pay attention to whether she is keeping to it. If she sees that she is not, she tries to figure out what went wrong.

Using the assignment book provided by the school, Suzanne carefully writes down the homework, and, before leaving school, checks to see that she has all the materials she needs to complete the work. At home, she does her work at the same time and place each day, checking off each task as it's completed so that she can see what's done and what she has left to do. She also plans when to start assignments that are due in a few weeks so that she doesn't feel rushed.

After the vignettes have been read, encourage the student to answer the questions on the **Comparison and Self-Assessment Questionnaire** (Figure 1). These questions require the student to make a comparison between himself and the students portrayed in the vignettes—that is, to see in what ways he is like Sam or Suzanne. Use the student's answers to help him understand his level of academic self-regulation skills.

1.3   Understanding Self-Regulated Learning

To continue helping the student increase self-awareness about the qualities and components of academic self-regulation, assist the student in completing the list of questions on Figure 2, the **Are You a Self-Regulated Learner?** handout (Cleary & Zimmerman, 2002), then discuss.

1.4   Understanding Academic Self-Regulation Tasks

Have the student read or ask the student to listen as you read the following case reports. Tell him to imagine that he is a "shrink" who is trying to understand how two clients, Andy and Olga, are feeling. Ask the student how he

FIGURE 1   Comparison and Self-Assessment Questionnaire

First, write a short description of how Sam or Suzanne acts or feels in relation to each characteristic. Next decide whether you think you are more like Sam or more like Suzanne.

Interest in schoolwork

Sam: _____

Suzanne: _____

I am more like   ☐ Sam   ☐ Suzanne

Level of effort

Sam: _____

Suzanne: _____

I am more like   ☐ Sam   ☐ Suzanne

Reason for trying (wants to, or is forced to?)

Sam: _____

Suzanne: _____

I am more like   ☐ Sam   ☐ Suzanne

Desire to be successful at school

Sam: _____

Suzanne: _____

I am more like   ☐ Sam   ☐ Suzanne

Ability to keep track of what he or she needs to do

Sam: _____

Suzanne: _____

I am more like   ☐ Sam   ☐ Suzanne

Desire to please teachers and parents

Sam: _____

Suzanne: _____

I am more like   ☐ Sam   ☐ Suzanne

FIGURE 2   Are You a Self-Regulated Learner?

Answer the following questions yes or no.

Do you . . .

1. Have a plan before you begin to do your schoolwork (what you will do, when you will start, where you will work, in what order you will do your work)? ☐ Yes ☐ No

2. Set a goal before you start working? ☐ Yes ☐ No

3. Visualize your goal and imagine how you might tell whether you are acting in the way that you want to act (that you are keeping to your standards)? ☐ Yes ☐ No

4. Create priorities (put your tasks in an order) and a schedule to do your work? ☐ Yes ☐ No

5. Think out specific strategies or ways to achieve your goals? ☐ Yes ☐ No

6. Expect to do well before you start doing your work? ☐ Yes ☐ No

7. Feel interested in the work? ☐ Yes ☐ No

8. Think the work is important or relevant? ☐ Yes ☐ No

9. Feel motivated to put forth as much effort as you can? ☐ Yes ☐ No

10. Feel able to stay focused while working? ☐ Yes ☐ No

11. Keep track of whether you are paying attention while you work? ☐ Yes ☐ No

12. Notice whether you are making progress toward being as successful at schoolwork as you want to be? ☐ Yes ☐ No

13. Try to figure out what you would do differently to help yourself improve? ☐ Yes ☐ No

14. See a relationship between how hard you work, your strategies, and how you actually do? ☐ Yes ☐ No

15. Self-correct and adjust your effort, revise your strategies, or ask for help if you see you are not doing as well as you want to do? ☐ Yes ☐ No

16. Give yourself a reward (for example, a compliment) or punishment (feel ashamed or self-critical) when you finish your work, depending on how you think you did? ☐ Yes ☐ No

From *Self-Regulated Learning: Practical Strategies for Struggling Teens,* by Norman Brier, © 2010, Champaign, IL: Research Press (www.researchpress.com, 800-519-2707)

would counsel them about the benefits of the three academic self-regulation tasks: setting goals, keeping track of what they have to do, and evaluating their performance to see whether they are accomplishing their goals.

Case Report A: Andy

Andy feels that he is like a song he once heard called "Nowhere Man." He has trouble paying attention at school, is almost always bored, and never finishes his work. As a result, he never hands anything in on time and is failing all of his classes. He has no confidence that he will ever be successful or will be able to get a job when he is older. When he thinks about success, Andy's heart starts to race and he feels very tired. Lately, even outside of school, he does not feel like doing anything. When a friend challenged him to a computer game, he quit when he started losing and then felt bad about doing that. His global studies teacher, a former police officer, seems to be an extra-good guy and has offered to sit down with Andy to figure out what he could do to make things better. So far, Andy has made excuses about why he can't meet with his global studies teacher.

Questions

1. Why does Andy feel like the "Nowhere Man"?
2. Does Andy have a clear goal?
3. Does Andy expect to succeed?
4. What are the feelings Andy seems to be experiencing, and how do these feelings seem to affect the chance that he will, in fact, become a "Nowhere Man"?
5. Does Andy seem able to plan, use strategies, self-evaluate, and seek help?
6. What do you think you might say to Andy to help him have hope so that he could be a "Somewhere Man"?

Case Report B: Olga

Olga was born in Russia and adopted when she was five years old by a family in the United States. She was always curious about Russia and, in particular, was fascinated by Russian skaters, especially after watching a Russian skater on television win the gold medal at the Olympics. Olga had never skated and wondered whether she would be good at it. She asked her mother to take her skating. Her mother was happy about that because she worried that Olga was too quiet and did not often ask for things that she wanted. Olga had never had a special hobby and was shy around other children, in part because she was very self-conscious about her accent. She usually spent her time outside of school alone.

Olga's mother took her to the ice rink. After watching the other people skate, some with the help of a skating instructor, Olga timidly and awkwardly tried. Her mother noticed how anxious and stiff Olga was. She was surprised, therefore, when Olga asked to come back next week for a lesson. Olga's mother told her that she thought it was a great idea and asked Olga to tell her more about why she wanted lessons. Olga explained that she kept thinking about how graceful the Russian Olympic skater was on television and said that she wanted to be like her.

Olga took a lesson, and, at the suggestion of the instructor, made a plan to take a series of lessons and set a goal. She and the instructor agreed to develop a skating routine that Olga would demonstrate in six months at a local skating show. It was open to young skaters at all skill levels.

Questions

1. How do you think the fact that Olga grew up in Russia affected her desire to ice skate?

2. How do you think that seeing the Russian Olympian skater affected Olga's wish to be a good skater?

3. Do you think Olga's interest in skating makes it very likely she will be a good skater?

4. How do you think Olga's shyness and self-consciousness might affect her chances of being successful at the upcoming skating show?

5. Do you think Olga needs an instructor, or do you think she should have—at least for a while—tried to skate on her own?

6. Do you think that having a routine and a goal makes it more likely that Olga will be successful? Why or why not?

Choice and Self-Determination

OVERVIEW

The ability and opportunity to make choices (particularly the choice to be self-disciplined) are essential elements of academic self-regulation. The interventions in this chapter focus on autonomy, as well as collaboration, willpower, stages of change, and use of a decision balance scale to facilitate self-regulation.

The Importance of Autonomy

To be academically self-regulated, students must have and exercise choice in selecting goals, setting performance standards, determining the level of effort they will expend, and picking the strategies they will use. Young people are more likely to take responsibility—and feel accountable for their academic behavior—if they appreciate the cause and effect relationships among intentions, decisions, and actions, and the consequences that result (Deci & Ryan, 1985; Skinner & Edge, 2002).

Making choices and having a sense of control are positively associated with increased motivation, feelings of self-sufficiency (Grolnick, Ryan, & Deci, 1991), and academic achievement, starting between grades 2 and 4 (Chapman, Skinner, & Baltes, 1990). Youth who believe that how well they do at school is based on their choices and actions perform academically better (Seligman, 1975), exert more effort, and are more engaged and persistent while learning (Skinner, 1995) compared to those who do not believe that their choices play an instrumental role in how they do at school.

The type of choices a young person makes is determined, in part, by her values and by what she believes is an important and desirable end state (such as seeing herself as a smart person or a person who gets high grades) or way of acting (such as being a person who is well-prepared or who always tries her best) (Rokeach, 1973).

The ability to consider the future is also important. To act in accordance with their values or "guiding principles," youth must be able to visualize how their values are manifested by their actions. Then they must establish goals and standards with those future reference points in mind. They also must periodically imagine this wished-for end state, examine their behavior, and determine whether their current actions match their aspired way of acting.

The Importance of Collaboration

Attempts to influence a student's sense of control and encourage him to make choices that facilitate academic self-regulation are more effective when presented as collaborations in which a rationale is presented along with the possible reasons a particular academic choice may have personal value. In a collaborative approach, directive, controlling language and attempts to persuade are avoided and the student's personal choices and perspective are emphasized. In addition, the ambivalence or discrepancies between how the student claims to want to act and how he is currently acting are noted, and any negative feelings he expresses about school or schoolwork are acknowledged (Deci & Ryan, 1985).

When working collaboratively, eliciting the student's consent to being advised in making choices about an academic goal is important, as is making clear whether any advice offered is acceptable to him.

The Importance of Willpower

A young person's willingness and ability to exert willpower play a key role in determining whether she will be successful in achieving her academic goals. Youth vary widely in this regard. Some make the decision, for example, to do their homework as soon as they get home and are able to maintain this commitment, while others are unable to meet a stated goal when faced with the opportunity to do something more pleasurable (Corno, 1993).

Studies of conscientiousness, which is considered to be an element of willpower, suggest that differences in temperament, or biologically based predispositions, contribute to a person's level of dependability, responsibility, and persistence (Costa & McCrae, 1992). Other factors that contribute to the ability and willingness to exert willpower include the degree of importance attached to a choice and the nature of one's expectations about the consequences of enacting—or not enacting—a choice (for example, whether the person will get caught, whether a punishment will be severe, whether a reward is valuable).

Stages of Change

The Transtheoretical Model of Behavioral Change (Prochaska, 1979) is helpful in understanding and assessing a student's readiness to exert willpower and act in an academically self-regulated manner. According to this model, a student's commitment to act in an academically self-regulated manner can be evaluated based on criteria linked to various stages of change.

A student in the first stage (precontemplation) has not formed an intention to act with greater self-control and either is unaware of the need to improve or considers the possibility of acting with increased self-discipline only when coerced or pressured. At the next stage (contemplation), the student is aware of the need to improve self-control but is unsure about her willingness to put forth the effort. A student at the third stage (preparation) has decided to try to improve and is either making efforts to do so or planning to make such efforts in the near future. At the fourth stage (action), the student is taking actual steps to improve and, in the final stage (maintenance), she is able to sustain the changes she has made.

It is not unusual for students to move back and forth through several stages before their actions become relatively stable.

The Decision Balance Scale

A decision balance scale can assist in identifying a student's stage of change (Janis & Mann, 1977). The student is asked to weigh the pros and cons of changing, including the concrete, instrumental, and anticipated psychological benefits and costs. The student is then asked to consider which benefits he feels are most important. Those answers will result in the scale's tilting either toward or away from a decision to make a change.

When the decision balance scale is used in combination with the stages of change model, youth in the precontemplation stage often decide that the pros of not working hard outweigh the cons of putting forth great deal of effort. Youth in the contemplation stage, on the other hand, usually see the pros and cons as relatively equal, while those in the action stage often see that the pros of working hard outweigh the cons (Prochaska et al., 2002).

INTERVENTIONS

2.1   Increasing Awareness of the Role of Choice (Part 1)

Most students, at one time or another, are likely to find schoolwork uninteresting, unimportant, or impossible to do well. As a result, they may feel "far away" or bored when at school and have little interest in setting academic goals or exerting effort when there.

Explain to the student that each of us has to decide what is important to us and what kind of person we want to be. This decision includes how we want to act at school, and, more specifically, whether we want to act with self-discipline and improve our academic performance.

Students are more likely to succeed in achieving an academic goal if they think that the goal is valuable and important and if they have a standard by which to define success. If they try only because their parents or teachers are pressuring them, they are less likely to be successful. Likewise, students are more likely to make progress if they choose on their own to apply willpower and effort, particularly when schoolwork seems uninteresting, unpleasant, pointless, or difficult.

Explain to the student that you are going to present a series of exercises that will help her improve her ability to do as follows:

- ► Make academic choices
- ► Experience a sense of control when doing schoolwork
- ► Adjust her level of effort
- ► Improve self-discipline

2.2   Increasing Awareness of the Role of Choice (Part 2)

The following two vignettes will help the student visualize and identify with the task of making choices and feel an increased sense of control over his academic behavior. Read or have the student read each vignette, then discuss the related questions.

Kari

Kari is somewhat obese and is self-conscious about her appearance, but she is very proud of how smart she is and how other kids seem to respect her answers. She wants to be on the high honor roll and works hard to do her best at school.

Her parents, though, are discouraged because they cannot get her interested in exercising or eating better. They constantly tell her what she should and should not eat, but it has little effect. On the other hand, they are proud of how well Kari is doing at school, and they let her decide when she will do her homework and how she will do it. When Kari brings home a good grade, they praise her and tell her how good she should feel because her academic successes are the result of her choices.

Questions

1. Why do you think Kari is able to work hard at school but not at changing her appearance?
2. Do Kari's parents treat her differently regarding her schoolwork and her appearance?
3. If you think they do, do you have a guess why?
4. What do you think might get Kari to consider doing something to improve her appearance?
5. Do you think if Kari's parents pressured her to do better at school, she would not try as hard?

Use the student's responses to highlight the relationship among interest, choice, and effort; how making choices allows a person to take credit for the outcome; and how being forced to do something often makes people unwilling to persist at a task or to put forth their best effort.

Juan

Juan's parents are very worried about being able to pay their bills and have to work many hours. As a result, Juan, who is their only son, is often on his own. When it comes to schoolwork, Juan believes in the "two-thirds rule"—he does two-thirds of his homework and feels okay if he gets a C. Juan likes making decisions and likes that his parents do not ask him a lot about school.

He often imagines what he will be like when he's older, and he pictures himself as a police officer. He doesn't think that you have to do great at school to be a police officer—as long as you pass, it will be okay.

When one of his teachers complained to the principal that Juan was lazy and never seemed to try his best, the principal called Juan to his office and yelled at him. Juan told the principal about his two-thirds rule and how he wanted to be a police officer. He explained that being a great student didn't matter to him. Instead of the principal complimenting Juan for his honesty or explaining how being a good student could help Juan be an even better police officer, or perhaps even a detective, the principal threatened Juan. He told Juan that if he did not display more effort at school, he would get a detention. Juan thought about what the principal said and decided that he would rather get a detention than do something he didn't want to do.

Questions

1. Do you think that Juan's two-thirds rule makes sense?

2. Do you think that the principal was right in trying to push Juan to adopt a new rule or standard?

3. Do you think it is good that Juan thinks about what he wants to do in the future as a way of deciding how he wants to do things right now?

4. What might the principal have done differently to get Juan to try harder?

5. Would you have defied the principal?

6. Is it good that Juan stuck with his own point of view?

Use the student's answers to highlight how making choices helps a person feel responsible for how things work out; how choices are usually based on what someone feels is desirable or important; and how it is helpful when people in authority encourage discussion, are sensitive to the student's feelings, and allow him to express both negative and positive feelings.

2.3 Assessing Awareness of Choice

It is important to be aware that one can exercise choice when making decisions about school. Tell the student you are going to read several statements and keep track of her answers, or give the student a copy of the **How Much Choice Do I Have?** handout (Figure 3). The student should indicate whether each statement is almost never true, sometimes true, or almost always true.

Discuss the student's responses. If her answers indicate that she thinks she almost always has some control over choices, ask her what feels good about taking responsibility for doing the work (for example, being praised for doing well) and what feels not so good (perhaps she is criticized when she "messes up"). If the student's answers reveal that she thinks she almost never has control over her choices regarding schoolwork, ask why she thinks so (for example, her parents want to be in charge or she did poorly in the past when she took responsibility) and whether she would like to have a greater say now. If she says yes, brainstorm some ways she might do so. Select one of the ideas and ask the student to be alert to her efforts in the coming week so that they can be discussed at the next meeting. Also ask the student whether she believes she has the willpower to be successful. Explain that willpower is the ability to keep working at a task, particularly when it is unpleasant or difficult.

2.4 Understanding Goals and Performance Standards

To continue highlighting how changing one's actions at school is a choice, ask the student whether he is considering making a change in either how he carries out his schoolwork or in how well he does at school. As part of the discussion, explain that the word *goal* means the end point or result of what

FIGURE 3   How Much Choice Do I Have?

Check the box that best shows how you feel about the statement.

	Almost never true	Sometimes true	Almost always true
1. I have a say in deciding when I will do my homework.	❑	❑	❑
2. I have a say in deciding how hard I will work.	❑	❑	❑
3. I have a say in choosing my strategies or plan for doing homework.	❑	❑	❑
4. When I get a grade, I believe how hard I try is a big part of why I do well or poorly.	❑	❑	❑
5. I think how well or poorly I do at school is mostly up to me.	❑	❑	❑
6. I can see the connection between what I do and do not do, and how well I do at school.	❑	❑	❑

From *Self-Regulated Learning: Practical Strategies for Struggling Teens,* by Norman Brier, © 2010, Champaign, IL: Research Press (www.researchpress.com, 800-519-2707)

you want to accomplish and the term *performance standard* means a detailed example that you can use to judge whether you are acting the way you want to act.

Ask the student the questions on the **Goals and Performance Standards** handout (Figure 4). Discuss the student's answers. Emphasize the importance of wanting to change because one sees value in changing, feels that he can change, and can learn from past attempts at change. If the student is willing, work together to develop a plan to make a small change in the way that he handles his schoolwork. At the next meeting, review his attempt to change, noting what worked and what barriers to change were present.

2.5 Highlighting the Relationship Among Choice, Willpower, and Effort

To help a student be more aware of the relationship among her perception of the usefulness of an academic task, her choices, and the effort she puts forth, ask her to describe a school task that she has been assigned but has not yet started.

Review the rationale behind the task, highlighting where possible the value or usefulness of the assignment to the student herself. Ask about and highlight the choices she has in doing the task. Clarify the student's point of view about the task and what, if anything, she might gain by doing it. Acknowledge any negative feelings and resistance that she might have about the task. Work together to devise ways she might complete the task, and, if she is willing, establish a specific goal—one that is somewhat challenging but doable.

Note and emphasize the student's interests, preferences, and sense of curiosity whenever possible in order to help her become aware of her motivation for doing the work. Use informational language only. Avoid using such words as *ought* and *should* or presenting approaches as if there is "a right way."

2.6 Monitoring Willpower

Ask the student to develop some "willpower indicators"—such as working for the amount of time intended, completing assignments, being prepared for what needs to be done at school, and avoiding distractions. Next, provide a copy of the **Willpower Barometer** (Figure 5). Ask the student to use the numbered line on the barometer to indicate, each day for a week, the degree to which he has maintained self-discipline and followed through on his positive intentions.

At the end of the week, review his scores. If they are relatively high, ask the student what helped make the score high (having a plan, following a routine, etc). If the scores are relatively low, ask what might have caused the low scores. Ask the student whether he would be willing to complete a Willpower Barometer for one more week. If so, ask him what scores he would like to shoot for and what indicators of willpower he wants to use.

FIGURE 4   Goals and Performance Standards

1. What are your school goals?

2. How can you tell whether you are doing okay at accomplishing those goals—are your goals clearly defined, and do they include specific performance standards with detailed strategies and time frames?

3. How well have you met your school goals and standards up to now?

4. Is there anything about the way you do your schoolwork that you would like to do differently?

5. If yes, what would you like to do differently?

6. How important are these changes or differences *to you?*

7. Will these changes positively affect your future?

8. What negative things might happen if you do not make these changes?

9. Do you think you are ready to change how you do your schoolwork now?

10. How can you tell?

11. Have you tried to change in this regard in the past?

12. If you have, what did you do that worked and what did you do that did not work?

13. Do you have confidence in your ability to change now?

14. Would you be willing to carry out an experiment to see whether you can act differently and what might get in the way of acting differently?

From *Self-Regulated Learning: Practical Strategies for Struggling Teens,* by Norman Brier, © 2010, Champaign, IL: Research Press (www.researchpress.com, 800-519-2707)

FIGURE 5   Willpower Barometer

Use the numbered line on the "barometer" to indicate, each day for a week, the degree to which you maintained self-discipline and followed through on your positive intentions.

Day 1

0	1	2	3	4	5	6	7	8	9	10

Day 2

0	1	2	3	4	5	6	7	8	9	10

Day 3

0	1	2	3	4	5	6	7	8	9	10

Day 4

0	1	2	3	4	5	6	7	8	9	10

Day 5

0	1	2	3	4	5	6	7	8	9	10

Day 6

0	1	2	3	4	5	6	7	8	9	10

Day 7

0	1	2	3	4	5	6	7	8	9	10

From *Self-Regulated Learning: Practical Strategies for Struggling Teens,* by Norman Brier, © 2010, Champaign, IL: Research Press (www.researchpress.com, 800-519-2707)

2.7 Explaining the Value of a Decision Balance Scale

Creating a "balance sheet" can help a student determine how much she wants to change (see the discussion of the decision balance scale earlier in this chapter). On the balance sheet, the student writes down the anticipated gains or benefits of making a change, along with any anticipated losses or costs of making the change (Janis & Mann, 1977). You might explain that a typical benefit is feeling pride in achieving a goal, while typical costs are the hard work that is usually necessary and anxiety about not being able to do as well as hoped.

Ask the student to select an academic goal that she has been considering but has not yet tried to achieve or one that she has tried but not with 100 percent effort. Present the **Decision Balance Scale** (Figure 6) and ask her to complete it, offering help as needed. When the scale is completed, review her answers. Discuss whether the decision scale tilts toward trying to change or not trying to change.

Ask the student to rate, on a 0 to 10 scale, with 0 representing the lowest possible number and 10 representing the highest possible number:

1. The importance to her of each of the reasons she gave to change.
2. The level of energy, or effort, the student feels she will have to put forth to be successful.

2.8 Assessing Stage of Readiness

To assess the student's readiness to exert willpower and try to change, ask him to complete the **Stages of Readiness for Academic Self-Regulation Inventory** (Figure 7). Provide help as needed, and ask him to rate each of the statements by indicating whether it is almost never true, sometimes true, almost always true, or always true. The letter(s) after the statement indicate which stage of change is likely associated with the answer, with *PC* for precontemplation, *C* for contemplation, *PP* for preparation, and *A* for action. The numerator is the tally of the endorsement of "almost always true" and "always true," and the denominator is the total number of possible endorsements associated with that state of change.

The student's responses can help you assess his readiness for change. When he has completed the inventory, ask whether he thinks the results are accurate and whether they are different from what they might have been a year ago. If he thinks the results are different, ask why. (Has he lost confidence? Does he find the work much more boring than he used to?)

2.9 Choosing Interventions Based on Stage of Change

To increase readiness to change, review the following list of tasks and select those that match the student's current stage of readiness, based on the results of the Stages of Readiness for Academic Self-Regulation Inventory.

FIGURE 6 Decision Balance Scale

Goal

_____

_____

Reasons to Work Toward the Goal

The benefits, or good things, that might happen if I try to accomplish the goal are . . .

1. _____

2. _____

3. _____

4. _____

Reasons Not to Work Toward the Goal

The losses, or bad things, that might happen if I try to accomplish the goal are . . .

1. _____

2. _____

3. _____

4. _____

FIGURE 7   Stages of Readiness for Academic Self-Regulation Inventory

	Almost never true	Sometimes true	Almost always true	Always true
1. There is nothing about my school behavior that I need to change. (PC)	❑	❑	❑	❑
2. Doing well in school is not important to me. (PC)	❑	❑	❑	❑
3. I try to spend as little time as possible doing my schoolwork. (PC)	❑	❑	❑	❑
4. I am bored when I do my schoolwork. (PC)	❑	❑	❑	❑
5. I can't see a point in learning what is being taught in school. (PC)	❑	❑	❑	❑
6. I know I have to work harder than I now do at school. (C)	❑	❑	❑	❑
7. I see that some of what is being taught will benefit me. (C)	❑	❑	❑	❑
8. I think about ways I can do better at school. (C)	❑	❑	❑	❑
9. I can imagine some good things that will happen if I do well in school. (C)	❑	❑	❑	❑
10. I want to learn even more about some of the things I am being taught. (C)	❑	❑	❑	❑
11. I am planning to study more. (PP)	❑	❑	❑	❑
12. I will fix up my work area. (PP)	❑	❑	❑	❑
13. I intend to keep track of what I have to do. (PP)	❑	❑	❑	❑
14. I will ask for help when I need it. (PP)	❑	❑	❑	❑
15. I am putting much more effort into studying. (A)	❑	❑	❑	❑
16. I am working hard at keeping my work area organized. (A)	❑	❑	❑	❑
17. I am keeping track of what I have to do. (A)	❑	❑	❑	❑
18. I am asking for help when I need it. (A)	❑	❑	❑	❑

Scoring

PC: ___ /5 = ___%   C: ___ /5 = ___%   PP : ___ /4 = ___%   A: ___ /4 = ___%

From *Self-Regulated Learning: Practical Strategies for Struggling Teens*, by Norman Brier, © 2010, Champaign, IL: Research Press (www.researchpress.com, 800-519-2707)

Precontemplation

For students predominantly in the *precontemplation stage,* the overall goal is to help them commit to acting with greater self-control:

1. Identify ways that school can have increased relevance and value to the student.
2. Help the student identify her core values and a vision of the future.
3. Find ways to connect the student's interests or hobbies to school tasks.
4. Identify some potential future rewards that might be gained if effort is applied.
5. Help increase feelings of self-efficacy.
6. Discuss the costs attached to changing, such as the need to exert a high level of effort, the necessity of delaying enjoyable activities, and feelings of discomfort that might arise. Problem-solve to reduce or eliminate these costs.

Contemplation

For students predominantly in the *contemplation stage,* the overall goal is to encourage greater effort in achieving academic goals:

1. Highlight discrepancies between the student's goals and values and his or her current actions.
2. Help the student imagine ways to feel proud of himself or herself in regard to school.
3. Help the student develop and practice using motivational self-talk.

   Encourage the student to regularly self-evaluate his or her progress at school.
4. Create possible strategies for change.

Action

For students predominantly in the *action stage,* the overall goal is to help them maintain self-discipline, learn to adjust their level of effort, and request assistance when needed:

1. Highlight the importance of willpower.
2. Use the student's aspired self-image as a standard and as a motivator.
3. Create self-rewards for engaging in desired behavior.
4. Establish or increase contextual support.

Maintenance

For students predominantly in the *maintenance stage,* the overall goal is to help them identify the risks of losing self-discipline and find ways to reduce those risks:

1. Identify triggers that could cause lapses in self-regulation.
2. Develop strategies to deal with lapses.
3. Highlight key aspects of the student's satisfaction with her "new" identity and identify the benefits and rewards of increased self-discipline.
4. Assess and support the student's beliefs about her ability to maintain the changes over the long term.

3

Understanding and Setting Goals

OVERVIEW

As noted in Chapter 2's discussion of the stages of change, improvements in academic self-regulation often begin when students undertake schoolwork with positive intentions to be more engaged, exert greater effort, and persist at school tasks, especially when bored or frustrated. Motivation, the willingness to move toward a goal by exerting effort, is needed to realize these intentions.

The Elements of a Goal

Goals can be distinguished from intentions by the inclusion of specifics, such as a clearly defined end point to signify success, a definite time frame by which the end point will be reached, and concrete strategies to accomplish the goal. As noted, setting a goal is an initial, essential step in self-regulation. The goal creates a structure to organize behavior, focus attention toward goal-relevant information and away from goal-irrelevant information, facilitate accountability, provide guidelines that assist in making judgments about how one is doing, create opportunities for feedback and self-correction, and provide a means to establish a set of markers to assess progress (Deci, Ryan, & Williams, 1996; Zimmerman, 2008).

Types of Goals

Goals can be distinguished in several ways. Goals can be distinguished by their intent—that is, by whether the desired end point is to achieve a positive outcome, such as being the best one can be at something, or to avoid or prevent a negative outcome such as failing or making a mistake (Higgins, 1997). Goals can also be distinguished by whether the goal is designed to impress others or to achieve a personally meaningful end. For example, some students may want to maximize favorable expectations and impressions and minimize negative ones, such as looking smart or being the best, while others may want to achieve a sense of mastery or increase their academic ability (Nicholls et al., 1989). The former type of goal has been described as an ego-involved or performance goal, and the latter as a task-involved, learning, or mastery goal (Dweck, 1986; Nicholls et al., 1989).

Ego-involved goals, or performance goals, at times interfere with academic self-regulation. Students who are very concerned about how they appear to others often concentrate too much on how well they are doing, feel anxious, and avoid challenges so as to not appear incompetent or less able than their peers (Elliot & Harackiewicz, 1996). Students who set learning or mastery goals, on the other hand, often have higher levels of academic self-regulation. They tend to focus on the learning process, more frequently seek help, and are more engaged and interested when doing schoolwork. As a result, those students usually attain higher levels of academic achievement (Dweck, 1986; Fryer & Elliot, 2008; Hagan & Weinstein, 1995).

Finally, goals can be distinguished by whether they are short-term or long-term. Short-term goals are thought to be more effective than long-term goals because feedback about one's progress is more immediately available (Zimmerman, 2008).

Independent of the type of goal, intentions and goals are more likely to be fulfilled when youth perceive the end point of the goal as useful, relevant, or important (Deci & Ryan, 2000; Eccles, Wigfield, & Schiefele, 2002). When they view the end point in these ways, learners are more likely to try to achieve the goal without external prompting, and they are more likely to feel engaged, initiate work on the school activity, display positive emotions while working (Skinner & Belmont, 1993), concentrate on the material (Csikszentmihalyi, 1988), exert effort, tolerate frustration, and persist (Linnenbrook & Pintrich, 2002; Zimmerman, 2008).

Time Perspective and Goals

The likelihood of fulfilling intentions and goals is also affected by one's time perspective. Students are more likely to fulfill intentions and goals when they consider the future and do not focus solely on the present. The ability to be oriented toward the future differs among youth. Some are able to take a relatively long perspective and anticipate a distant future, while others have a relatively short perspective and experience difficulty anticipating future events.

Students who can consider the future tend to be better at academic self-regulation. They are better at creating images of possible payoffs that might result if they achieve their goals. As a result, these students can use their images of future benefits to justify the hard work that is often necessary to attain a future payoff. In addition, images of future benefits provide a means to tolerate the aversive feelings and the sacrifices that often arise when one defers meeting immediate needs for a future reward (Zimbardo & Boyd, 1999). The need to concentrate on a future payoff is especially important if the payoff is far away because the value a student attaches to a task decreases as the anticipated incentives to be derived from performing the task are delayed (Simons et al., 2004).

The ability to be oriented toward the past also differs among youth. The ability to consider the past facilitates academic self-regulation because it allows them to problem-solve when necessary, and it can potentially increase feelings of self-efficacy in achieving success (Bandura, 1997).

INTERVENTIONS

3.1 Identifying Key Elements of Intentions and Goals

To help the student clarify the key elements of intentions and goals and be able to distinguish between the two, ask her to complete the **Key Elements of Intentions and Goals** handout (Figure 8).

Use the student's answers to highlight the following key points:

► An *intention* is a desire to do something, while a *goal* adds specifics, such as a clear end point, the details of what is to be accomplished, and strategies to accomplish the end point.

► It is important to identify any challenges that have prevented success in the past, including a lack of faith in one's ability to be successful and a belief that the intention or goal is not important.

► Intentions and goals are more likely to be accomplished if future payoffs, as well as things that worked or did not work in past attempts, are considered.

3.2 Understanding the Nature of a Goal

Ask the student to do the following:

1. Define the word *goal*. Use his answer to emphasize that a goal is the finishing point of a journey, a way to mark an ending, the object of one's efforts, and/or a desired end.

2. Describe two goals that he has set. Review his goals to see whether he has a defined end point and a time frame for judging when he reaches the end point.

3. State whether the goals were achieved and what he used as indicators of success.

4. Describe, if he accomplished both goals, what he did or did not do that helped him be successful. If he did not accomplish either or both goals, ask him what prevented his success and what he might do differently next time.

3.3 Distinguishing and Identifying Goal Types

Explain to the student that academic goals can be sorted into different types based the outcome that the goal is designed to achieve. Academic goals, for example, can be classified as either positive or negative, such as whether the goal chosen is not to fail (negative) or to make personal progress (positive). Tell the student that you are going to describe two pairs of students who have different types of goals. Explain that after you present the examples, you are

FIGURE 8 Key Elements of Intentions and Goals

Read the questions and answer by checking yes or no or writing in the spaces provided.

1. Have you made a "good intention" or promise ☐ Yes ☐ No
   to yourself, either on New Year's Eve or after getting
   back a bad grade on an exam (such as "I will try harder"
   or "I will do my homework").

2. Did you follow through on your good intentions ☐ Yes ☐ No
   or promises?

3. Have you had good intentions and then carefully ☐ Yes ☐ No
   thought out: (a) how you would know if you were
   accomplishing these intentions, (b) the time frames
   that you would use to accomplish what you
   intended to accomplish, and (c) the specific strategies
   that you would use to succeed?

4. Did you expect to be successful or unsuccessful? What did you base your prediction on?

   _____

   _____

5. Did you consider how valuable or important these ☐ Yes ☐ No
   intentions were to you before you began?

6. Did you consider past attempts to work on these ☐ Yes ☐ No
   intentions, things in the present that could help or
   hurt the success of your attempt, and/or future good
   and bad things that would result if you were or were
   not successful?

7. How do you think considering the end point of an intention, a time frame to
   accomplish the intention, and strategies to achieve the intention might help you
   determine if you will be successful in making an intention a reality?

   _____

   _____

8. How do you think the importance of an intention affects the likelihood of
   achieving the intention?

   _____

   _____

From *Self-Regulated Learning: Practical Strategies for Struggling Teens,* by Norman Brier, © 2010, Champaign, IL: Research Press (www.researchpress.com, 800-519-2707)

Figure 8 (p. 2 of 2)

9. How do you think your expectations or predictions about your ability to succeed affect the likelihood that you will accomplish your intention?

_____

_____

10. How do you think considering the past, present, and future affect your likelihood of success?

_____

_____

11. Do you think considering one "time zone" (past, present, or future) is more important than considering another time zone? Please explain.

_____

_____

going to ask her to identify the type of goal demonstrated in the example and will ask her which types of goals she usually sets.

Read or have the student read, then discuss the following pairs of descriptions, one at a time.

Toni and Rafael

Toni usually gets in trouble at least once a week for coming late to class. At the start of each day, she almost always says to herself that she will not be late, then she meets a friend in the hall, starts talking, and loses track of time. She is now grounded for one week and has promised her mother that she will not be late to class again.

Rafael has never been good at anything in school except spelling. For reasons he doesn't understand, he is a great speller and gets 100s on almost every test. He hears that there is going to be a citywide spelling test and that the winner is going to get a prize. He gets especially excited when he hears that the prize is going to be the new iPod that just came out.

Questions

1. What was the specific end point or goal that Toni and Rafael each wanted to achieve? Were their goals positive or negative? (A positive goal might be to win a prize, while a negative one might be to avoid getting into trouble.)

2. Which type of school goals do you usually try to set—ones that achieve a positive outcome or ones that avoid a negative outcome?

Marla and Sam

Marla loves learning about the solar system, so her father bought her a telescope. Every night she would go on the roof of her apartment building and spend hours looking at the sky. This year in science, she is going to learn about astronomy. She cannot wait for the class to start and plans to work as hard as she can so that someday she can be an astronomer.

Sam knows that he is the smartest student in math class. He loves getting the best grade on tests, especially when most of his classmates do poorly. The teacher tells Sam that he is the only student in the class who will be allowed to take an honors math class. The teacher says that the honors class will challenge Sam and allow him to increase his math skills even more. Sam can't wait to tell the other students and see their reactions.

Questions

1. What was the specific end point or goal that Marla and Sam each wanted to achieve?

2. When you set a goal, is it to learn about something that you are interested in, make personal progress, achieve something positive in the future, outdo others, and/or get a reward?

3.4 Setting an Academic Goal

Explain to the student that you will work together to help him set an academic goal that he thinks is interesting, valuable, or important, using the guidelines that have been discussed so far.

First, ask the student to create a mental image of how he wants things to be when he completes the goal. Encourage him to be as specific and descriptive as he can so that another person could use his description to determine how well he was making progress or when he had achieved the goal. Emphasize that the more specific he is about his goal, the more likely he will achieve it. Therefore, he should include as many details as possible to describe the end point.

Second, ask the student to imagine a path between where he is now in regard to the goal and where he wants to end up when the goal is accomplished. Work with him to identify steps along the way that will help him reach the end point. Ask him to place the steps in the order that he needs to perform them.

Third, for each step identified, ask the student to establish a time frame by which to achieve it, as well as a time frame by which the overall goal will be achieved.

Now ask the student to complete the **Goal Planning Questionnaire** (Figure 9), which will help him evaluate the quality of his goal planning.

Review the student's answers with him and use them as necessary to clarify or improve the goal and thereby increase the likelihood of his success in meeting it. Encourage the student to start working toward the goal and be ready to evaluate his progress at the next session.

3.5 Maintaining Motivation

Ask the student whether she knows any people who, once they make up their mind to do something, always get it done. If she can identify someone, ask her what she thinks that person does (or does not do, such as procrastinate) to be so successful in achieving goals. If the student cannot think of such a person, describe someone who is industrious, determined, and employs good planning skills. Include in your description examples of strategies that a successful "goal-achiever" might use (for example, writes down the goal, regularly checks progress, sets aside specific times to work toward the goal).

Now ask the student to think about some of her attempts to achieve academic goals, and, with these attempts in mind, ask her to answer the questions in the **Goal Achievement Questionnaire** (Figure 10).

FIGURE 9   **Goal Planning Questionnaire**

Think about the goal you have set, then read the questions and write your answers in the spaces provided.

1. Did you choose the goal because someone in authority told you to, or because you wanted to?

2. Do you believe that the goal is important? If so, why?

3. Is the end point of your goal specific and measurable? If so, how?

4. Does the end point of your goal involve personal progress or acquiring a specific target, such as a grade? If so, please explain.

5. Do you think that the goal is challenging but doable (not too easy but not too difficult)?

6. Do you have specific strategies to achieve the goal? If so, what are they?

7. Do you have a way to monitor if you are making progress? If so, how?

8. Do you have someone available who can help you achieve the goal if you run into trouble accomplishing it? If so, who?

FIGURE 10   Goal Achievement Questionnaire

Read the questions and answer by checking yes or no.

When you have tried to achieve an academic goal in the past, did you . . .

	Yes	No
1. Think about giving yourself a reward if you did what you hoped to do?	☐	☐
2. Try to figure out how you could "stay on task" and accomplish your goal by thinking of ways not to be distracted by other things that seem more fun (such as playing on the computer)?	☐	☐
3. Talk to yourself while working to remind yourself of the reasons for doing your work?	☐	☐
4. Encourage yourself to notice what you are doing well?	☐	☐
5. Try to make the work as interesting and enjoyable as possible?	☐	☐
6. Break up the work into sections to help make the goal seem more doable and prevent boredom?	☐	☐
7. Make a plan for when you get off track and are not working well to help you get back on track?	☐	☐
8. Think about what you have done in the past that helped you be successful and tried to do the same things again?	☐	☐

After she has completed the questions, use her answers as a springboard to discuss the following:

- ► The value of self-rewards
- ► The need to reduce or avoid competing personal goals
- ► The value of self-talk
- ► Strategies to prevent boredom and giving up
- ► The importance of examining past successes

Factors Influencing Goals

OVERVIEW

Goals are influenced by a number of factors, including a student's expectations about the likelihood of success, as well as the value the student places on the school task and the level of interest the student has in the task. Interventions in this chapter are designed to tap into these three areas.

Expectations

Expectations or predictions about the likelihood of achieving an academic goal strongly affect intentions, motivation, and self-regulation (Zimmerman et al., 1992). Students' predictions about the likelihood of success on an academic task are typically based on their perceptions of past academic achievements, self-confidence, the perceived difficulty of the current academic task, and the perceptions, attitudes, and expectations of parents and teachers (Wigfield & Eccles, 1992). Developmentally, children at the beginning of elementary school are overly optimistic about success. They expect that they nearly always will do well on a task, even if they have failed to do so in the past. The expectations of young children, therefore, seem to be based on hope rather than prior performance. Over the course of elementary school, children's expectations are increasingly affected by their academic successes and failures, and, as a result, correspond more and more to their actual performance (Wigfield & Eccles, 1992). In addition, by about age 13, youth begin to view ability as a limiting factor in achieving desired goals and no longer feel that greater effort alone is sufficient for success (Nicholls, 1990).

A student's expectations strongly affect his persistence. A student who expects to succeed but fails tends to intensify his efforts and persist until successful. On the other hand, if he expects to fail, believing that there is a large discrepancy between his current level of skill and the standard that he has to achieve, he tends to become discouraged when he begins to do poorly and typically ceases to try (Bandura & Cervone, 1983).

Avoidant behavior is also very common among youth who have low expectations for success (Covington & Beery, 1976). At times, a student's avoidant behavior is an attempt to protect his sense of self-worth. Thus, when he tries a school task but fails, he protects his self-esteem by attributing the failure to a lack of effort or to the boring, irrelevant nature of the school material. As a result, he is less likely to feel self-critical. On the other hand, if he attributes his failure to a lack of ability, especially a lack of ability that he sees as a permanent "flaw" (such as low intelligence), he is likely to feel self-critical and inadequate (Harackiewicz, 1979; Wigfield, 1994a, 1994b).

Value

A student's intentions, motivation, and academic self-regulation are also affected by the value he attaches to a school task (Wigfield & Eccles, 1992). To put forth a high level of effort, the student must view a task as interesting (Eccles & Parsons, 1983), relevant (Wigfield, 1994a, 1994b), desirable in terms of the anticipated incentives (Rokeach, 1973), or important (Battle, 1965). When these attributions are present, the student is motivated to complete the task. When these attributions are absent, the student has a negative feeling about the task and is not likely to complete it. Thus, these attributions create either a positive or negative feeling (Feather, 1982) that powerfully influences whether the student will begin working on a task (Pintrich & DeGroot, 1990) and whether he will sustain his effort and self-control to complete it (Feather, 1988).

The degree of value a student attaches to a school task is affected by these factors:

► His self-image and goals

► The costs (such as not seeing friends, being tired) and benefits (such as making progress, getting a reward) anticipated as a result of the academic activity

► How he has felt in the past when engaging in the activity (for example, the level of enjoyment experienced; feelings of novelty, challenge, or stimulation)

► The degree of value attached to the activity by people with influence over the student, such as parents, teachers, and friends

► The extent to which he has been successful in the past while doing the task

► The perception that the activity is relevant and important, based either on its relationship to an existing interest or to a future goal

► Expectations about the probability of success (Eccles & Wigfield, 1995; Wigfield, 1994a, 1994b; Wigfield & Eccles, 1992)

Although feelings of self-efficacy are important, a student is more motivated and self-regulated when tasks are highly valued, even if he thinks the probability for success is low. Conversely, a student is less motivated and self-regulated if the tasks are seen as having little value, even if he thinks the probability of success is very high. When a student values a task, he is more likely to choose to perform the task—and to perform it well. On the other hand, when a student does not value a task, particularly when he perceives that the cost of doing so is very high, he tends to avoid working on it (Battle & Wigfield, 2003).

Interest

The level of interest a student has for a school task also plays an especially important role in determining the amount of value he will attach to a task, the goals and strategies he will select, the degree of attention he will maintain, and the degree of academic success he will achieve (Hidi & Ainley, 2002; Mitchell, 1993). Level of interest has been found to account for about 10 percent of the variability in children's academic achievement, based on an analysis of studies conducted in 18 different countries (Schiefele, Krapp, & Winteler, 1992).

Having a high level of interest promotes academic achievement by increasing positive mood, a sense of engagement, a focus on benefits rather than costs while learning, curiosity, attention, effort, persistence, and retention (Hidi & Harackiewicz, 2000; Sansone & Thomas, 2005). Conversely, a lack of interest in a school task increases the likelihood that a student will focus on the costs rather than the benefits of completing the task, quit working, persist but feel stressed by feelings of disengagement, and attempt to change the activity to make it more interesting (Hidi & Ainley, 2008; Sansone, Wiebe, & Morgan, 1999).

Developmentally, children initially value academic tasks based on the degree of interest, pleasure, or enjoyment that they experience while engaging in an activity. Over the course of elementary school, the value children attach to a task becomes distinct from interest, and they become influenced by what they believe the important adults in their life consider valuable. By late elementary and middle school, children attach value to a school task primarily based on their perception of its usefulness (Wigfield, 1994a, 1994b; Wigfield & Eccles, 1992).

INTERVENTIONS

4.1   Clarifying Expectations About Academic Success

Explain to the student that expectations or predictions about how successful she believes she will be at a school task strongly affect how much she will want to work at the task and the amount of self-control she will demonstrate. Tell her that you will ask a series of questions to help her be more aware of her usual expectations about school success and how these expectations affect her actions.

Ask the student the questions on the **Expectations and Actions** handout (Figure 11). Use the student's answers to highlight the following key points:

► Expectations are predictions or anticipations.

► Past academic achievements, self-confidence, perceived difficulty of a task, and the opinions of others affect these anticipations or predictions.

► Expectations affect effort and persistence.

4.2   Understanding How Value Is Attached to a Task

Explain that beliefs about what is good or desirable (that is, what we value) help people decide whether they want to make an effort to achieve something, and, specifically, to decide what they want to achieve. Tell the student that everyone often finds several things to be valuable at the same time and that these values might conflict. For example, a student can find it valuable to socialize with his friends on the computer. At the same time, he might think it is valuable to avoid getting into trouble for not completing a school assignment. He then has to choose which activity has more value. Tell the youth that you are going to describe two students who are faced with a "value conflict" and that you are going to help him be more aware of what he values by asking what he would feel and do in the same situations.

Read or ask the student to read the following, then discuss.

Austin's and Toni's Value Conflicts

Austin is confused. On the one hand, he promised the other kids he would get on the computer at 7 P.M. to play a game with them—a game that has been especially exciting lately. On the other hand, his mother says he is becoming a computer addict and that she is going to take him to a psychologist for help. He has been getting in trouble a lot lately for not getting his schoolwork done on time and has an essay due tomorrow that the teacher assigned a week ago.

Toni's favorite teacher in her new school is giving a test at the end of the week on all the material they have covered so far. The teacher said that the test score would determine 50 percent of their grade on the next

FIGURE 11 Expectations and Actions

Read the questions and answer by checking yes or no or writing in the spaces provided.

1. Are you good at correctly predicting how well you will do   ❑ Yes   ❑ No
   on a test or on your report card?

2. When you guess incorrectly, are your guesses usually too high or too low?

   _____

3. When you expect to do well, how do you feel, and how does this feeling affect your
   level of effort on the task that you are about to do?

   _____

   _____

4. When you expect to do poorly, how do you feel, and how does this feeling affect the
   level of effort you show for the task?

   _____

   _____

5. What types of information do you use to form your predictions about the likelihood
   of success or failure (for example, past performance, the opinions of others)?

   _____

   _____

6. Do you feel that how you did in the past on a similar task is   ❑ Yes   ❑ No
   the best predictor of how you will do in the future?

7. Do you feel that your level of effort is the best predictor of   ❑ Yes   ❑ No
   howyou will do?

8. Do you feel that how important or interesting you find the   ❑ Yes   ❑ No
   task is the best predictor of how you will do?

9. In making a prediction about how well you will do on a task, do you mostly consider
   your last grade, how well you have usually done in the past, the specific characteristics
   of the task, and/or how well prepared you were?

   _____

   _____

10. Do you think it is good or bad to think a lot about how well you are going to do? Why?

    _____

    _____

11. Do the predictions of others (parents, teachers, friends) affect   ❑ Yes   ❑ No
    your predictions about how well you will do?

From *Self-Regulated Learning: Practical Strategies for Struggling Teens,* by Norman Brier, © 2010, Champaign, IL:
Research Press (www.researchpress.com, 800-519-2707)

report card. Toni really wants to do well and was planning to study a lot, but as she is leaving school, Samantha invites her over. Toni does not have many friends in the school, and Samantha seems really nice.

Questions

1. What is the value conflict in each situation?
2. Which things seem important or valuable to Austin and Toni?
3. What would you do if you were Austin and Toni?
4. If Austin and Toni decide to do their schoolwork, do you think their value conflicts will affect their ability to do the work well by interfering with their persistence or ability to focus?
5. What might be some ways Austin and Toni could decide what to do?

Use the student's answers to highlight the following key points:

► The relationship between values and choices

► The importance of anticipated incentives and consequences

► The importance of interest and enjoyment

► The challenge of working effectively in the face of a value conflict

4.3 Clarifying How Expectations and Value Affect Self-Regulation

Tell the student that to better understand her school expectations, ways of deciding about what is valuable about doing schoolwork, and how these decisions affect her actions, you are going to have her fill out the **Expectations and Value** handout (Figure 12). Ask the student to read each statement and indicate whether it is usually true or false.

Use the student's answers to highlight the following key points:

► Predictions have a powerful impact on effort.

► Being confident is associated with trying harder.

► A lack of confidence is associated with avoidance.

► Importance, relevance, and interest in a task increase its value.

► At times, value is determined by balancing anticipated costs and benefits.

4.4 Attaching Value to a Task (Part 1)

Explain to the student that it is generally easier to attach value to a school task if he has a good reason—a rationale—as to why the task might be useful and is allowed to express his thoughts about doing the task, including any negative thoughts and feelings about doing it. Tell the student that you are

FIGURE 12   Expectations and Value

*Read each of the statements below. If you agree with the statement, circle **T** for true. If you disagree, circle **F** for false.*

1. When I am confident that I can do my schoolwork, I make an effort to do well. T   F

2. I avoid doing my schoolwork if I think I will get a poor grade. T   F

3. When my parents or a teacher says a school task is very important, I try harder. T   F

4. If I think I won't get in trouble if I don't do my work well, I don't make much of an effort. T   F

5. I do not do the best I can at my schoolwork because I don't see how what I am learning is useful. T   F

6. I do not always pay attention in school because what we learn is often boring. T   F

7. I do my schoolwork because I want the teacher to be proud of me. T   F

8. I like to learn at school because a lot of what I learn is interesting. T   F

9. I do not try my best at school because I don't think that what I learn has anything to do with what I will do in the future. T   F

10. When I think that good things will happen if I do well in school, I try harder. T   F

going to describe two teachers who have assigned a school task. You will then ask whether he thinks that his willingness to do the task would change depending on which of the teachers assigns the task.

Read or have the student read the following two descriptions.

Mr. Smith

Mr. Smith is a tall, strongly built man with a powerful voice. He acts like he is still a sergeant in the army, which he was before becoming a social studies teacher. He loves talking about wars, and without asking the class what they would like to do or what their preferences might be, lists the main battles of the Civil War and goes around the room making assignments. He tells the students that they are to describe a battle that he has picked for them in as much detail as possible, including the specific date of the battle, the number of soldiers involved, and the number of soldiers who died. One student raises his hand and asks whether he could switch the battle he was assigned to another battle. Mr. Smith says no. Another student raises his hand and asks why it is important to include the number of soldiers who were involved in the battle and the number of soldiers who died in it. Mr. Smith says, "Because I think it is important. Just do what I ask you to do."

Mrs. Liskowitz

Mrs. Liskowitz is a quiet, gentle woman who is extremely enthusiastic about the books she discusses in her English class. She explains to the class that each student is to pick a book from the bestseller list of the local paper. She tells the class the reason she feels this assignment is important is that it will give them an idea of what books are most popular so that they can decide whether the books considered most popular are, in fact, the books that should be considered good literature. She hands out the list of best-selling books, along with a brief description of each, and asks the students to select the book that seems most interesting to them. When one student complains that the books on the list are too long, she listens patiently, states that she understands that not everyone loves to read, and repeats again why she thinks the assignment is important.

Ask the student how he feels about each teacher's approach in making the assignment. Would that affect how he would do the work? Use his answers to emphasize the following points:

► The importance of choice and its relationship to value and interest

► That value and interest are associated with tasks being perceived as meaningful and related to personal interests

► That feelings of choice, value, and interest are associated with increased effort and engagement

4.5   Attaching Value to a Task (Part 2)

Ask the student to tell you about an important task that a teacher has assigned recently. Then ask the following questions about the task:

1. Did the teacher clearly explain the purpose or usefulness of the task?

2. If the teacher has, do you agree that the task is useful, important, and/or interesting?

3. How much of an effort, on a scale of 0 (no effort) to 10 (maximum effort) do you plan to make?

4. Is the amount of effort you intend to put forth based on how useful you think the task is, your level of interest in it, and/or any consequences that you think might happen if you don't do it?

5. If you don't think the task is useful, is there still a specific benefit of doing it? If so, what is that benefit (for example, you might learn something interesting or your mother might stop criticizing you)?

6. If you don't think that the task is useful or interesting but feel that you have to do it well, what could you do to increase your motivation? Can you think of ways to make the task more relevant or interesting?

Use the student's responses to highlight the following:

► The relationship between effort and perceptions of usefulness, importance, and interest

► The need to balance the benefits of doing an academic task with the costs of not doing it

► The need to try to make an uninteresting school task more relevant and interesting

4.6   Increasing Interest in a Task

Using comments made in prior discussions, discuss the relationship between the student's feelings of interest in a school task and the amount of effort and self-control he puts forth while working on it.

Ask him to describe three topics that he has learned about this past week. For each topic, ask the student how he felt when the topic was being discussed in class:

► Interested?

► Curious?

► Involved and able to see a relationship between the topic and something that he thinks is interesting or important?

► Bored?

Ask the student how his degree of interest, curiosity, involvement, and engagement affected his level of effort and persistence. If he felt uninterested and bored but did not want to get in trouble, did he come up with any ideas or tricks to help him pay attention and get the work done? For example, did he do any of the following:

1. Give himself a reward, or receive one from someone else, if he did the work?

2. Try to think of ways that performing the activity was good for him or think about the costs of not doing the work?

3. Make the topic more interesting by thinking about how he could relate the activity to something he is interested in or likes to do?

4. Try to obtain help and encouragement from someone to maintain motivation?

5. Try to work with others to make the work more enjoyable?

Use the student's responses to highlight these key points:

► The relationship between interest and value

► The relationship between interest and the level of attention and effort given

► The relationship between interest and enjoyment

► Ways to problem-solve when uninteresting tasks need to be done, including using rewards, considering benefits and costs, and finding connections between the task and activities that are interesting or enjoyable

Planning, Effective Strategies, and Help Seeking

OVERVIEW

The interventions in this chapter focus on the essential skills of planning and using specific strategies likely to improve academic outcomes. A third factor in academic success, adaptive help seeking, is also targeted.

The Importance of Planning

Students who are adept at academic self-regulation know how to plan. They take time to select strategies or tactics carefully, in part to ensure that their strategies are appropriate to their goal and sufficiently specific to achieve the goal correctly and completely (Zimmerman, 2008). In addition, they take time to consider whether the goal needs to be divided into its essential subcomponents, and, if so, they consider which strategies or tactics best match each of the subcomponents. They also take time to organize the subcomponents and their matching strategies into a sequence that includes time frames for tracking progress (Pressley & Woloshyn, 1995). Finally, they consider ways that they can sustain their motivation and willpower until the goal is achieved (Wolters & Rosenthal, 2000). Academically self-regulated students are proactive; they tend to be more committed to employing their strategies, exert greater effort while doing so, and are more persistent compared to reactive learners, who tend to be impulsive and either do not plan or use unfocused plans that lack specific strategies (Paris, Byrnes, & Paris, 2001).

Attributes of Effective Strategies

Successful strategies include the when, where, and how of what needs to done. Students are more likely to accomplish an academic goal when they can identify strategies that have worked well in the past, can use these strategies in a relatively automatic manner, and are able to transfer these strategies to similar tasks (Paris & Byrnes, 1989). In addition, when a plan is not working well, students are more likely to accomplish an educational goal in an academically self-regulated manner if they can flexibly revise the elements of their strategy or change the entire strategy when necessary (Winne, 1997).

Developmentally, children as early as the preschool years are able to perceive means–end relationships and can develop strategies to remember objects and events. Thus, they can be goal-oriented, think instrumentally, exert effort, and understand the purpose of a strategy (for example, "If I practice, I will remember better"). In addition, with guidance, children as young as preschool age can also selectively apply a strategy, and, when necessary, revise the strategy or select a new one (Paris & Byrnes, 1989).

Help Seeking

Academically self-regulated students tend to be particularly skilled in using the strategy of seeking help to achieve educational goals. They have higher expectations for school success and higher rates of achieving academic goals when they ask for help if they need it (Newman, 2008). Students adept at seeking help think before making a request for help, and, in particular, consider whether their request is necessary, what they should say, and whom and when they should ask for help (that is, they usually ask after they have made a genuine effort on their own). In addition, students adept at seeking help are usually active learners, and, as a result, they prefer that the person giving assistance provides suggestions rather than answers (Newman, 2008).

Starting around the middle years of elementary school, students view teachers as potentially helpful sources of assistance, particularly if the teacher conveys an awareness that the student has a problem, is perceived as interested in giving advice, gives students the opportunity to make an effort on their own to solve the problem, and encourages them to ask questions. At around this time, students also become increasingly aware of the potential costs of asking for help, such as feeling embarrassed in front of their classmates or feeling incompetent. As a consequence, they begin to weigh the benefits against the costs of seeking help before making a request for assistance (Newman, 1990).

INTERVENTIONS

5.1   Increasing Awareness of Planning and Choosing Strategies

Explain to the student that you are going to describe two students who are about to start to work on an important academic goal. Tell her that you will then ask which of these students is most like her.

Warren

Warren knows that he can usually get his work done, even if he waits to the last minute. He really wants to get good marks and impress the teachers. He comes close to that goal but often messes up by not getting his assignments in on time or not doing them exactly the way the teachers wanted him to. For example, last week, he received a poor grade on an essay he was assigned to write on a chapter in his social studies book. There were too many pages to read by the time he remembered to look at the assignment, and he was not able to finish the reading in time. He had not known what to do, so he guessed on some of his answers. When he got the essay back, aside from the errors he made because of his wrong guesses, he saw that he had not followed the instructions and had left out a lot of the other information that the teacher wanted everyone to include. His teacher keeps telling him that if he is going to get a good grade, he has to start his work right away, make a plan, and keep track of how well he is carrying the plan out. Warren knows she is right, but usually he either forgets to do his work or does something he would rather do, until the teacher mentions it or his mother reminds him to do it.

Juanita

Juanita's mother is a teacher. From the time Juanita was in first grade, her mother taught her to ask herself, when given an assignment, how she might do the assignment before she begins. Although Juanita is a good student, she would like to make even more progress this year, especially in English, the class her mother teaches. Therefore, when Juanita is given a book report as an assignment, she pays careful attention to when the report is to be handed in, and she thinks a lot about the different ways that she could do the assignment really well. She looks carefully at the teacher's guidelines and thinks about what has worked in the past when she had done well on similar assignments. Juanita makes a plan and writes down each of the tasks that she needs to do and the order in which she will do them. She also makes a schedule for doing the work and feels proud that she is, as her mother calls it, "mapping"—that is, creating a path between where she is now in her work on an assignment and where she needs to be when she is done.

Use the student's responses to highlight the importance of the following:

► Thinking or reflecting before getting started

► Looking carefully at the teacher's suggestions and guidelines

► Considering the effectiveness of past methods that have been used

► Creating a written "map" that includes the tasks to be done, the order they should be done in, and the schedule that will be followed

► Seeking help and flexibly changing a plan, if necessary

5.2 Increasing Awareness of Forethought and Evaluation in Selecting Strategies

Explain to the student that to be an effective learner, it is necessary to think before getting started, carefully consider the goal that he wants to achieve, and identify the strategy or strategies that are most likely to lead to success. Explain, further, that in selecting strategies, effective learners pay careful attention to the directions and suggestions that the teacher provides, as well as their prior use of strategies to see which ones have worked best.

Ask the student to pick a school task that he has to perform regularly, such as learning a set of spelling words or completing a set of math computations. Help the student identify two strategies that he could use to complete the task (for example, in spelling, he could read the list over and over and try to remember how the words look, or he could ask someone to say the words aloud for him to spell; for math, he could ask a parent to do the math assignment with him, or he could start on his own and ask for help if needed).

Help the student articulate any strategies that his teacher has recommended and to recall whether the teacher explained why the strategy is a good one. Ask the student to state his goal in accomplishing the task and to suggest what he thinks would be a good method to achieve the goal. Ask him why he chose this method (for example, it was the easiest or it's a way he will learn the most).

Ask the student to imagine that he is a scientist and has the job of finding out which strategies are best. Ask him to use one strategy for an upcoming task and to use another strategy on a subsequent occasion when he is asked to do the same task. Once both strategies have been tried, ask him to describe the results and whether he thinks one strategy worked better than the other.

Use his answers to highlight the importance of evaluating and modifying strategies based on his goals and the effectiveness of the strategy when he used it.

5.3   **Enhancing the Link Among Goals, Strategies, and Self-Reflection**

Remind the student that a goal is an end point or destination that she is trying to reach when given an academic task. The end point is usually both practical (for example, to get the work finished and done well) and personal (for example, to feel proud of oneself or get a reward). People generally believe that the best way of getting somewhere is to know where they want to go and how they will get there. Further, the more detailed the "map" they use, the less likely it is that they will get lost. Therefore, students who consider when, where, and how they will achieve their academic goals are usually more successful.

Explain that a person on a journey might run into roadblocks and have to find a different path or method to reach the destination. Good learners, therefore, need to be flexible—that is, they need to be able to switch strategies when necessary. Explain to the student that to help her relate strategies to goals, you want her to pick a long-term assignment that she has recently been given and then describe the practical and personal goals and the methods or strategies that she used—or is using if she is still working on the assignment.

Ask the student whether she did any of the following:

1. Used the strategy in the past. If so, ask her how well it worked and how she judged its effectiveness in helping her reach her goal (for example, was the strategy easy to carry out? Did it result in a good grade?).

2. Considered in detail when, where, and how she would carry out her strategy.

3. Changed the strategy a little bit, or even entirely, because it was not working. If so, ask how she realized that the strategy was not working (for example, did she feel lost? Was the assignment taking forever to finish?).

4. Sought help to get the assignment done, and if so, did getting help result in a change of strategy?

Use her answers to highlight these key points:

► The importance of connecting strategies to goals

► The value of reviewing the effectiveness of past methods

► The importance of noting when, where, and how a strategy is to be carried out

► The need for flexibility

► The value of assistance

5.4 Facilitating the Use of Adaptive Help Seeking

Explain that learners who are able to seek and obtain help when they are stuck in trying to achieve an academic goal are more likely to eventually achieve their goal, compared to those who need help but do not seek it. Also explain that seeking help is more likely to lead to success if a student takes the time to consider these ideas:

► Whether his request is necessary

► Who would be the best person to ask

► What he should say when making the request

► The best time to ask

► The nature and extent of help he wants (such as hints to get started, or the answers)

Tell the student that you are going to describe a student who has to decide whether he should ask for help. After you read or have the student read the description, ask the student for his opinion about what he thinks Marcus ought to do.

Marcus

Marcus was stuck. He did not understand what the math teacher, Mrs. Jones, was saying and had tried to raise his hand to ask, but he put it down when two things happened. First, the teacher said, "Not now, Marcus. I do not have the time to answer any questions." Then John, who sits behind Marcus, made fun of Marcus for raising his hand. Marcus knew that without help, he would not be able to do the homework and also that Mrs. Jones would believe, like she always does, that he is a bad kid who just doesn't care. His friend Tiffany saw that Marcus had tried to raise his hand, heard Mrs. Jones' answer, and told Marcus to follow her out of the room to see whether he could ask her for help in the hall. Eddie, another friend of Marcus's, overheard Tiffany's advice and said, "Don't do that. Wait for the right time to ask Mrs. Jones for help, and think about how you want to ask. Or, because Mrs. Jones seems to always be in a rush, maybe there is someone else you could ask who really would want to help you."

Questions

1. Why did Marcus stop asking Mrs. Jones for help? Would you have asked your question in that situation?

2. Do you think that Tiffany offered good advice?

3. How can someone tell whether it is okay to ask a teacher for help?

4. Did Eddie offer good advice?

Use the student's answers to highlight:

► The importance of help in accomplishing a goal

► The need to consider who to ask and what to ask for

► The importance of how you ask and when you ask

6

Self-Concept and Sense of Efficacy

OVERVIEW

The ability to set goals, willingness to expend effort to reach them, and investment in monitoring progress is strongly affected by students' academic self-concept and expectations in regard to academic success. These academic self-representations create a framework that students use to interpret and organize academic experiences; to define what is pleasurable, valuable, important, and relevant to learn; and to gauge the value of persistence and doing well. Academic self-representations have an especially strong impact on students' predictions about the likelihood that effort will bring academic success and on their willingness to approach learning tasks and persevere until completion (Eccles & Parsons, 1983).

Academic Self-Concept

All of us have a picture in our minds of how we are as students. For example, we have a picture of how skilled we are in different subjects or how intelligent we are. Our academic self-concept, or picture of ourselves as a student, and the self-judgments we attach to this picture are based in large part on the feedback we get from others and on our past school successes and failures. We often use these self-pictures to decide whether we will be successful on a school task or willing to try something new or hard. We also use these pictures to decide whether something is going to be fun or interesting and to determine how we feel about our performance on a task in school. We form images of ourselves not only in regard to how we believe we are now, but also in regard to what we think we ought to be and would like to be in the future.

The term *self-concept* refers to a person's self-representations or self-perceptions. A young person's self-concept evolves from her observations and evaluations of immediate experiences and from the feedback she receives from important people in her life (Marsh, 1992; Wolfe, 2003). These self-representations include beliefs about how she is now, as well as what she believes she ought to be and might be in the future (Higgins, 1987; Markus & Nurius, 1986; Markus & Wurf, 1987).

Studies of youths' self-concepts indicate that they tend not to have a unitary or global self-concept; instead, their self-perceptions are often multi-faceted and typically can be divided into academic and nonacademic (social, emotional, and physical) domains (Marsh & Seeshing, 1997). The quality of a student's academic self-concept is strongly related to the level of her academic achievement and only weakly related to the nonacademic components of her self-concept (Marsh & Seeshing, 1997). Within the academic domain, there are also distinct subcomponents. For example, students typically have distinct self-concepts about math and English. Thus, mathematics achievement is substantially correlated with math self-concept but not English self-concept, while English achievement is substantially correlated with English self-concept but not math self-concept (Marsh, Byrne, & Shavelson, 1988).

How students decide whether they are proficient in an academic domain contributes to the nature of the associations between their academic achievement in that area and their self-attributions in regard to that particular subject. According to one popular theory, students make two types of determination: an external comparison between their own academic skills and the skills of other students in a specific academic subject, and an internal comparison between their own skills in one subject and their skills in another subject. When making an internal comparison, students are likely to evaluate themselves differently for different academic subjects ("I am great in math but stink in English"). Further, students who view themselves as having a very high level of academic skill in one particular academic subject are more likely to evaluate themselves as having a relatively lower academic self-concept in other academic subjects (Marsh, 1992).

Developmentally, young children tend to have relatively positive academic self-concepts, in part because they do not relate their self-perceptions to objective information and have fewer opportunities for social comparisons and limited ability to make use of the comparisons that they can make (Jacobs et al., 2002). As they get older, their academic self-concepts become more stable and more strongly associated with actual academic achievement. In addition, as they become older, students are increasingly aware of others' level of competence and where they fit in the ability hierarchy (Jacobs et al., 2002; Marsh et al., 2005). As a result, students' academic self-concepts tend to decline in varying degrees across academic domains and steeply decline in middle childhood and early adolescence, ages at which they frequently make social comparisons (Jacobs et al., 2002).

Self-Perceptions About Ability and Intelligence

At times, youth do develop global academic self-representations, based largely on their explanations of why they have succeeded or failed at schoolwork. These self-representations about general ability are likely to be low if a student attributes past failures to internal and stable causes, such as lack of ability, and are likely to be high if a student attributes past academic successes to controllable causes, such as effort (Weiner, 1986).

Self-representations, or core beliefs, about intelligence in particular strongly affect the quality of a student's academic self-regulation. Students who believe that they are born with a fixed amount of intelligence are likely to feel that their intelligence is unchangeable. When they perform poorly in school, especially after exerting a high level of effort, they tend to believe that their poor academic performance indicates a lack of ability. As a result, they are more likely to be self-critical and self-conscious, give up or avoid difficult school tasks, make excuses, and avoid seeking help. Students who believe, on the other hand, that their intelligence or ability is malleable are more likely to be motivated. They are likely to believe that it is possible to make incremental, positive changes in ability, especially if effort is applied. As a result, they tend to undertake challenging learning tasks, display initiative, exert a high level of effort, try out a variety of learning strategies, and concentrate (Dweck & Master, 2008; Ommundsen, Haugen, & Lund, 2005).

Academic Self-Concept and Academic Self-Regulation

A positive academic self-concept has motivational or energizing properties (Marsh et al., 2005). Students who see themselves as academically competent are more confident. They expect to succeed, and, as a result, they put forth effort and persist, even if they initially have difficulty. When these students do succeed, their academic success further enhances their academic concept and motivation—and the likelihood of future academic success (Deci & Ryan, 1985; Harter, 1992). In addition, students who have a positive academic self-concept are more likely to have high academic standards. They are more likely to avoid engaging in negative behavior that interferes with their academic goals, monitor their academic performance, and compare their academic self-perceptions to their actual academic behavior and use the feedback to take corrective actions (Higgins, 1987).

The nature of students' academic self-concept—and self-perceptions of competence in particular academic domains—affects their level of interest in those academic domains (Wigfield et al., 1997). When students see themselves as competent in an academic task, they are likely to attach greater value and interest to it and spend more time on it. Further, while working, they are likely to experience an increased desire to learn and higher levels of pleasure while doing so. As a result, they display higher levels of concentration and persistence. In contrast, students who see themselves as incompetent at an academic task tend to attach little value to it, spend less time on the task, feel less engaged while working, and demonstrate less improvement (Hidi & Ainley, 2002; Jacobs et al., 2002).

Self-Efficacy and Academic Expectations

A student's expectations about academic success are determined partly by the nature of his academic self-concept and partly by the degree to which he feels capable or efficacious while doing schoolwork (Bandura, 1997). Efficacy beliefs, in turn, are influenced by the student's interpretations of past accomplishments, perceptions of how similar past accomplishments are to the task that is about to be attempted, and beliefs as to whether he has the necessary capabilities and personal control to be successful (Bandura, 1994, 1997).

Affective reactions also influence a student's sense of efficacy. Optimism, calmness, and a positive mood increase feelings of self-efficacy, and the self-efficacious feelings, especially if associated with academic success, further enhance optimism, calmness, and a positive mood. A despondent mood and anxiety lower feelings of self-efficacy, and a lack of feeling efficacious, particularly if associated with academic failure, further enhances a despondent mood and increases anxiety while doing schoolwork (Bandura, 1997; Linnenbrook & Pintrich, 2002; Schunk, 1996). Providing encouraging information about the likelihood of academic success increases feelings of self-efficacy and positive mood, but these feelings are not likely to be sustained if failure occurs after the encouragement (Bandura, 1977).

Self-Efficacy and Academic Self-Regulation

Expectations for success and feelings of efficacy, as noted, increase a student's motivation to work toward an academic goal, the degree of interest she has in attaining a goal, and the level of effort, persistence, diligence, and engagement she demonstrates while working (Bandura, 1997; Eccles & Parsons, 1983). Students with high levels of self-efficacy in a particular academic domain, while working at tasks in that domain, experience higher levels of self-determination, set higher aspirations in that domain, show greater strategic flexibility, are more accurate in their self-evaluations, are more willing to take on challenging tasks, and are more willing to self-monitor learning outcomes (Bouffard-Bouchard, 1990; Knee & Zuckerman, 1998; Newman, 1990; Zimmerman, 1989b).

Students who do not feel efficacious expect to do poorly; as a result, they are unmotivated, make attempts to avoid the task, exert relatively little effort while working, and fail to persist (Bandura, 1982; Försterling, 1985). In addition, they often develop feelings of "learned helplessness"—believing that nothing they do will affect how successful they will be (Seligman, 1975). These students do not believe that effort will be sufficient to attain success, especially if they attribute past failures to personal deficiencies considered to be stable and enduring (Dweck & Rapucci, 1973). They are also prone to academic self-handicapping—that is, to protect their self-esteem and influence how others judge them, they deliberately create an alternative explanation for their anticipated failure. In this way, they have an excuse for not doing well and hope, as a result, to avoid looking stupid. Such students often create excuses by their actions (such as socializing rather than doing the homework) as well as by their inactions (such as not studying for a test). Students who engage in academic self-handicapping tend to have higher levels of anxiety and lower levels of academic self-regulation (Covington, 1992; Thomas & Gadbois, 2007).

INTERVENTIONS

6.1 Explaining the Key Elements of Academic Self-Concept

Explain that you are going to read or have the student read a short passage from the diary of Sarah, who is upset about how she sees herself as a student. Tell the student that after you read the description, you will ask her some questions about whether she thinks that Sarah's feelings are accurate.

Sarah's Diary

Dear Diary:

I failed the third math quiz in a row. The teacher said it was a very hard test and that most of the kids in the class would not do so well. Jasmine and Sharon did very well, though. They both got over 90. I never do as well as them. My friend Jane tried to be kind when she saw that I was upset. She said, "You will do better next time." I bet she really thinks I am stupid. My math teacher saw I was upset, too, and also tried to be kind. As I was walking out of class, he said that even though I did not pass, I should be proud of myself because I was improving. He went on to say that he thinks it's because I am working hard and meeting with Mrs. Sebastian each morning for extra help. Maybe I am making progress, but it sure feels bad to keep failing. What is the point? I might as well stop trying. My mother keeps saying that I am smart and that I ought to be doing better. It makes me so mad. I am trying my best. I can't figure out why I am not getting good marks. I was good in math in second grade, and I do really well in English. I wish I could get the same marks in math.

Questions

1. How does Sarah see herself as a student?
2. What information does Sarah use to judge herself?
3. Should Sarah compare herself to how she used to do or to others, or should she judge herself based on her personal progress?
4. Should she give up?
5. Should she base how she ought to be on her mother's beliefs?
6. Is it good or is it bad that Sarah wishes that she were as good in math as she is in English?

Use the student's responses to the questions to emphasize these key points:

► The importance of being objective—for example, noticing that the teacher said it was a hard test and that most students would not do well

► The benefit of focusing on personal progress and not on comparisons to others, especially others who excel

► The importance of recognizing that most people are good at some things and less good at others and that one's level of ability in an academic subject (such as math) can change

► The importance of trying and not giving up, especially when you can learn new strategies to do better

6.2   Clarifying the Nature of Academic Self-Representations

Tell the student that to help him determine how he pictures himself as a student, it is helpful to answer two sets of questions. Provide or ask the questions on the **Academic Self-Representations** handout (Figure 13).

Use the student's responses as a basis to discuss the following:

► The words or terms that he uses to describe himself as a student

► Whether those words or terms are based on objective information and are fair and balanced

► The effect of feedback on self-representations

► The importance of focusing on personal progress

► That most students have different pictures, or concepts, of themselves for different academic areas

► That most students compare themselves to other students, and they also compare their own abilities in different subjects

► That students become more self-critical as they get older because they develop the ability to pay more attention to facts and to judge how they are doing compared to others

6.3   Demonstrating the Relationship Between Self-Attributions and Academic Self-Concept

Explain to the student that we form pictures of ourselves as learners based on our self-attributions—the meanings and judgments we attach to how well we do based on our direct observations of our own behavior. When students attribute how well they are doing in school to something they can control, such as effort, they are more likely to feel hopeful about doing better, and they tend to try harder. When they attribute their academic performance to something they cannot control (for example, their ability) or base their self-judgments on comparisons with the performance of others, they are more likely to feel discouraged and try less hard.

Next, explain that the meanings we attach to success and failure influence our self-judgments. After a success, we are more likely to establish and monitor new academic goals if we focus on the skills that helped us succeed

FIGURE 13   Academic Self-Representations

1. What do you most notice about yourself when you are at school (for example, you try hard, you are usually bored, you never pay attention)?

2. What do you most notice when you do homework (for example, you put it off, you work hard)?

3. How do you judge yourself at school and when doing homework? Do you say good things, bad things, or both? What specifically do you say to yourself?

4. Do you focus on what you do right, wrong, or both?

5. What do you hear your teacher, other students, and your parents say about you as a student?

6. How do these comments make you feel?

7. Do others focus on what you do right, wrong, or both?

8. Do you mostly compare yourself to others in deciding whether you are doing okay?

9. Do you mostly compare yourself to how you did at an earlier point in that class?

Put a check mark beside any of the descriptions that are true for you, compared with others of your age.

❏ I am good at English language arts.

❏ I am good at math.

❏ I get good grades in English language arts.

❏ I get good grades in math.

❏ I find work in English language arts classes easy.

❏ I find work in math classes easy.

❏ I feel hopeless when it comes to English language arts.

❏ I feel hopeless when it comes to math.

❏ I have always done well in English language arts.

❏ I have always done well in math.

❏ I believes overall I am a good student.

❏ I believe I have been a better student in the past than I am now.

From *Self-Regulated Learning: Practical Strategies for Struggling Teens,* by Norman Brier, © 2010, Champaign, IL: Research Press (www.researchpress.com, 800-519-2707)

and the amount of effort we made. On the other hand, after a failure, we are more likely to establish and monitor new goals if we focus on alternative strategies we could use and changes we can make in our level of effort.

Finally, tell the student that you would like to ask her some questions to help her be aware of the attributions she makes. Begin by asking her to think of a time she did well on a test and a time when she did poorly. Ask the following questions:

1. For the test you did well on, why do you think you did well?
2. For the test you did poorly on, why do you think you did poorly?
3. Do you think that you can control how you well you will do the next time you take tests like these, either by changing your strategies and/or your level of effort?

Use the student's answers to highlight:

▶ The importance of increasing effort, seeking help, and using different strategies

▶ The importance of not judging yourself based on qualities you cannot control, such as ability or luck

▶ The need to concentrate on what you *can* control

6.4 Being Aware of Feedback and How It Affects Self-Attributions and Effort

Explain that the comments and reactions of teachers, parents, siblings, and other students strongly influence how we see ourselves and how hard we work at school. Positive comments and reactions increase our confidence, and negative comments and reactions make us feel discouraged and lose motivation.

Ask the student what happens when he receives either a very good or very bad test grade:

1. What do your teachers, parents, siblings, and peers typically say about the grade?
2. Do you think that what those people say is what they *really* feel about your performance on the test? How can you tell whether the feedback is honest?
3. Whose comments about your performance affect you the most?

Then ask:

1. When you have done well, how do people's comments about your ability, effort, and strategies affect you?
2. When you have done poorly, how do people's comments about your ability, effort, and strategies affect you?

Use the student's responses to highlight:

► The value of feedback that focuses on a student's effort and use of strategies

► That feedback focusing on ability and other things that cannot be controlled causes discouragement and lack of motivation

► The importance that feedback be appropriate to the student's level of performance (that is, not giving disproportionate or undeserved praise)

Now, ask the student to pick an adult he believes has a strong level of confidence in him—someone who always expects that the student will do okay at schoolwork if he tries. Ask who the adult is and what the adult says and does. Then ask the student to remember a time when the adult was complimentary and encouraging before he started a school task. Did the encouragement help him:

1. Feel calmer when he did the task?
2. Be more willing to try the task and put forth effort while working?
3. Keep working on the task until it was finished?

Use the student's responses to highlight these concepts:

► The power of other people's judgments

► The effect of encouragement on mood and effort

6.5 Facilitating an Incremental View of Intelligence

Ask the student to think of a recent time when she received a grade that was either especially good or especially bad. Then ask these questions:

1. Did your parents, teachers, or peers comment on your overall ability ("You are so smart!" or "What is the matter with you?"), or was the comment about your actions ("You really made a lot of effort!" or "Why didn't you try something else when you got stuck?")

2. Do you think that your grade was the result of your natural ability (that is, something you were born with), the amount of effort you made, and/or the strategies you used?

Using her responses as a guide, explain that after getting a lot of poor grades, students sometimes think they are stupid and believe that their academic difficulties mean that they lack intelligence and—because of this "permanent deficiency"—will always do poorly. That is, they think that their level of ability is unchangeable. As a result, they are self-critical and self-conscious, often do not see the point in making an effort to improve, and either avoid doing their work or put forth very little effort.

Tell her that scientists have found, though, that abilities *can* be improved if a student is motivated to work hard, seek help, and use effective learning strategies. Explain to the student that you are going to present a story that highlights how ability can be increased through effort, the use of effective learning strategies, and practice.

Kuo

Kuo came from China at age 9. He is now 14. When he first came to the United States, his English was very poor and he was often teased. As a result, he felt embarrassed and avoided being around other children. A kind teacher—who, coincidentally, had come to the United States at around the same age as Kuo—wanted to help him. The teacher suggested that Kuo get help speaking English properly from an acting coach he knew. Kuo liked the suggestion, worked with the acting coach, put forth a great deal of effort to improve, kept experimenting until he found the right strategy, and eventually succeeded. Now he can speak without an accent and is no longer teased.

Ask the student what part of the story stands out to her. Use her responses to reiterate that ability is changeable with effort, help, and use of good strategies.

6.6 Understanding How Academic Self-Concept Affects Expectations, Interest, and Effort

How we see ourselves as students is usually based on our past performance on a school task. That perception, in turn, influences our predictions about how successful we will be on similar tasks and the amount of confidence we have when doing a task. In addition, how we feel when doing a task affects our predictions about success. Optimism and calmness, for example, increase self-confidence, while sadness and anxiety lower it. At times, predictions about the likelihood of failure—and anxiety about these predictions—can cause someone to avoid doing schoolwork, feel defeated and helpless, or make excuses to "save face."

Explain to the student that you want to help him see how his own expectations about performance affect his success. Ask him to describe, in as much detail as possible, a time when he was assigned an extremely difficult school task. When he was about to start the task, did he think about any of the following:

1. Times when he faced a similar difficult task and how well he did then

2. What his parents, teachers, or other students said about how he did on the task

3. How he felt while doing the task (anxious, calm) and how those feelings may have affected his confidence and his expectations about success

Then ask the student to answer these questions about the difficult task he completed:

1. How did you actually do on the task?

2. Were your predictions accurate and based on a correct reading of the facts?

3. Do you think that your predictions were balanced (that is, based on all the available information, both positive and negative)?

4. Do you think that your performance on the task was the result of your particular abilities? Your actions? Both?

5. Did the comments of others affect your predictions, confidence, and effort?

6. Did your feelings while doing the task affect your predictions, confidence, and effort?

Use the student's answers to highlight the following:

► How perceptions of past performance on similar tasks influence current predictions about success

► How predictions about the likelihood of success and the feelings a student experiences while doing an academic task influence self-confidence

► How predictions influence the importance a student attaches to a school task

► How predictions influence the level of effort a student puts forth while doing the school task

► The importance of checking to see whether predictions are based on facts and balanced

6.7 Being Aware of Avoidance and Self-Handicapping

Explain that when a young person lacks self-confidence, predicts failure, feels helpless, and worries about looking stupid, she may try to create an excuse instead of trying her best. That way, if she fails, it will appear to be a result of not trying rather than being inadequate or stupid. Explain that the strategy of making excuses to avoid anticipated negative judgments of others is called *self-handicapping,* which can be self-fulfilling—that is, self-handicapping guarantees failure because the student does not do the work necessary to succeed.

Tell the student that, to determine whether she is at risk of self-handicapping, you are going to ask her a series of questions (based generally on Urdan and Midgley's [2001] self-handicapping scale). She should answer yes or no to each question.

Ask, "When you don't think you will do well on a school test and want to have a reason to explain why you won't do well, do you . . ."

1. Put off studying until the last minute?
2. Let your friends keep you from paying attention?
3. Purposely not try hard?
4. Get involved in a lot of activities so that there is little time to study?
5. Goof around the night before?
6. Make up some excuses you could give to others, such as "I was not feeling well" or "I had to do something with my parents"?

Use the student's responses to highlight:

► The self-defeating nature of self-handicapping

► The importance of remembering that abilities can change with increased effort, assistance, and the use of carefully selected strategies

7

Self-Guides and the Possible Self

OVERVIEW

The self-representations that form an academic self-concept can motivate a student to maintain actions consistent with her valued self-attributions and avoid actions that are perceived as inconsistent with those self-attributions. Thus, self-representations can provide both an organized set of characteristics that a student can use as a "self-guide" (Higgins, 1991) or performance criteria and a desired set of end points or goals that can energize her toward attaining an aspired "possible self" (Markus & Nurius, 1986). A student's positive possible self provides a target to strive for, and a negative image becomes something to avoid. The student's level of perceived self-efficacy plays an important role. When a student's perception of self-efficacy is high, she is likely to be confident about her ability to regulate her thoughts, actions, and mood. She also is more likely to successfully monitor her activities and be more confident about achieving short- and long-term goals (Bandura, 1982; Schunk & Pajares, 2002).

Self-Guides

Young people create self-guides, or self-directive standards, by visualizing and articulating the ideal ways they can act and the negative behaviors and attitudes they want to avoid. Once these self-guides are created, a student can juxtapose his actual behavior with the behavior that he ideally wants to engage in or feels that he ought to engage in (Higgins, 1987). In this way, he can evaluate the degree of match between his desired behavior and values and his actual behavior. If there is a discrepancy, the student can use this feedback as a prompt to reduce the discrepancy. According to Higgins (1991), self-guides facilitate academic self-regulation most when they are:

▶ *Salient*—and therefore relatively accessible and easy to follow

▶ *Coherent*—so that the standards that make up a self-guide can convey an organized picture of what is considered desirable

▶ *Directional*—so that the desired, positive outcomes are clearly indicated

Appraisals by significant adults, such as teachers and parents, play a key role in determining whether a student will focus on his ideals or will focus on what he feels he *should* do. Adults who primarily emphasize ideal behaviors tend to increase the likelihood that the student will create self-guides based on hopes or aspirations. Adults who primarily emphasize "shoulds" or "oughts" increase the likelihood that the student will create self-guides based on a sense of duty or obligation (Higgins, 1991).

The quality of the interaction between adult caregivers and a student affects the likelihood that the student will adopt and adhere to the self-guides that have been promoted by the adults. Youth who have responsive and sensitive caregivers are more likely to acquire self-guides, and these self-guides are more likely to strongly influence their behavior, presumably because caregiver influence is matched to the student's needs and wishes and is more frequent and consistent. Uninvolved caregivers are less likely to have a strong effect on a student's self-guides, probably because they are more likely to ignore the young person's actual needs and wishes and are less likely to attempt to influence the student's behavior. Over-permissive or over-protective caregivers are also less likely to strongly influence a student's self-guide because their feedback tends not to be appropriate to the student's needs, desires, and actual performance (Higgins, 1991).

Academic Self-Concept and Future Time Perspective

As discussed, the academic self-representations that make up a student's academic self-concept are based not only on the student's views of her past and present achievements but also on her possible self—that is, her anticipations, images, and hypotheses about how she may be, and would and would not like to be, in the future (Nurmi, 1991). These images also include the student's perceptions of her duties or obligations, as well as her perceptions of the people she values and devalues (Higgins, 1987; Markus & Nurius, 1986).

As has also been mentioned, youth differ both in their willingness to attend to the future and in their ability to do so. The latter is partly a function of age. Younger children are less able to consider the future and are less interested in doing so, while adolescents are better able to imagine future events and are more interested in doing so (McInerney, 2004). Young people are more likely to attain their possible selves—and to avoid acting in ways inconsistent with their ideals—when they believe that these future self-representations are attainable, realistic, acceptable, and valuable and when the significant adults in their life feel the same way (Markus & Nurius, 1986; Oyserman et al., 2006). The level of a student's perceived self-efficacy plays an important role in determining the extent of her aspirations, as does the degree of flexibility the student is able to display when selecting strategies to attain her possible self (Bouffard-Bouchard, 1990).

Self-Guides, Possible Selves, and Academic Self-Regulation

Academic self-guides and possible selves thus are imagined, self-directive actions that allow a student to mentally simulate or rehearse future events, thereby facilitating planning, problem solving, and self-control (Pham & Taylor, 1999). By creating a detailed image of the future, the student is better able to set priorities and define what is relevant, salient, and important to focus on. In addition, the presence of a defined possible self creates a framework to organize the student's goals into a coherent whole and to create a script to connect her thoughts to her actions. As a result, the student is better able to relate her strategies and actions in the present to potential outcomes in the future, to sequence events, and to evaluate whether her plans are viable. In addition, as a result of linking long-term actions and goals with present actions, the student is likely to increase the incentive and instrumental value she attaches to present actions and goals (Miller & Brickman, 2004; Pham & Taylor, 2008), which in turn increases the likelihood that she will display enhanced effort, task persistence, self-monitoring, problem solving, and self-correcting behavior (Markus & Nurius, 1986; Markus & Wurf, 1987; Oyserman & Terry; Pham & Taylor, 1999).

Mental simulation or rehearsal in regard to a student's possible self is especially helpful in facilitating academic self-regulation when the mental simulation includes concrete steps the student might enact to become the person she wishes to be. By considering the near as well as the distant future, the student is able to create a sequential series of subgoals, or steps—that is, a path that she can follow from the present to the future (Oyserman et al., 2004; Pham & Taylor, 1999). With such a path, the student is more likely to perceive the future as tangible and attainable. In addition, the presence of a path, composed of a series of identifiable markers, makes it more likely that the student will monitor her progress, feel efficacious, and correct any discrepancies between where she currently is on the path and where she wishes to be (Pham & Taylor; 1999; Zimmerman & Bandura, 1994).

Academic self-guides and possible selves also influence academic self-regulation by affecting the type of emotions the student is likely to experience. When a student is able to match her behavior with the performance criteria that comprise her self-guide and possible self, she is more likely to feel happy, hopeful, and competent and to demonstrate effort and persistence. When a student fails to act in ways that match her aspirations, she is more likely to feel sad, discouraged, and incompetent and to demonstrate less effort and persistence (Higgins, 1991).

INTERVENTIONS

7.1 Clarifying the Nature of a Self-Guide

Explain to the student that it is helpful to visualize and put into words—as clearly and completely as possible—the ideal ways in which he would *like* to act and not act, and the ways that he feels he *ought* to act and not act. To picture what these actions might be, the student can consider his current actions and how they differ from what he has pictured as desirable ways of acting. If the student observes that he is not acting in the ways he wishes to, he needs to picture alternative actions that more closely approximate what he sees as desirable behavior. Once these alternative behaviors are identified, the student should mentally rehearse the behavior and then try to match the behavior using his mental self-guides.

Explain that by using a set of standards or self-guides, people are able to judge the amount of progress they are making toward achieving their ideal behavior and can be more aware of any discrepancies between their actual behavior and their wished-for behavior. They are then able to use this information to make corrections.

Tell the student that in order to highlight the elements of a self-guide, you are going to present the following story and some related questions.

Tim's Story

Tim was excited. He was finally going to go to a public school. After six years at St. Regis Elementary School, he won't have to wear a uniform, can talk in the halls, and won't have to hear over and over what he ought to do and not do to be a good person.

Tim was tired of always fussing with his homework and spending so many hours making sure that it was accurate and complete. He had heard from his friends who go to public school that you could fool around and not always hand in your work, and that nothing much happens. Unlike at St. Regis, in public school you are just given a warning and then you have time to fix whatever you did wrong.

As he entered the public middle school and finally found his homeroom class, Tim was surprised. The teacher standing against the wall at the side of the class sure didn't look like the teachers he was used to at St. Regis. This teacher looked big and scary. When all the students were in their seats, the teacher began to talk. He said his name was Mr. Reilly. He wanted to first tell a little about himself and then talk about what he expected from them this coming year.

He explained that this was his very first day of teaching. Before becoming a teacher, he had been a marine for eight years. When he left the marines, he didn't know what he wanted to do, but he did know that he liked to be part of a group where people worked together to try to do their best, were loyal to each other, put forth their best effort to achieve a goal, and did not give up until they were successful.

Mr. Reilly explained that he had seen a commercial for the program "Teach for America" and thought teaching would be a good fit for him, so he signed up for the program. Now, two years later, here he was. He told the students that he was going to be their social studies teacher as well as their homeroom teacher and that he would work hard to prepare lessons that were interesting and important to them. He also said that he hoped they would come to see that they could count on him for help. He would always do his best to answer their questions, and, if they wanted, they could meet him before the start of class for extra assistance.

Mr. Reilly then said he wanted all the students to tell a little about themselves—specifically, how they should act this year if they want to feel proud of themselves and to believe that they are acting how they and their parents believe that they ought to act. He said that students should also mention any ways of acting that they should try *not* to demonstrate. Mr. Reilly suggested, for example, that they might think of specific ways they had acted in fifth grade that they want to change or improve, as a way of picking something they should do this year to help them feel proud of themselves.

After listening to Mr. Reilly, Tim was confused. He thought that Mr. Reilly seemed like a good guy and wanted Mr. Reilly to like and respect him. The idea of goofing around this year now seemed kind of dumb. Much to Tim's surprise, when it was his turn to talk, he told everyone what he had been thinking—that he had gone to a private school and wanted to fool around at this new school, but now thought that it wasn't such a good idea.

At least for right now, Tim said, he wanted to picture himself as someone who keeps track of his homework. Last year, he told his fellow students, he would often get in trouble for forgetting to do his homework, doing it wrong, or forgetting to hand it in. This year, he wanted to make sure that he brought home the stuff he needed to do for homework each day, do it really carefully, get it done on time, and remember to hand it in. When Tim finished, Mr. Reilly thanked him for his honesty and said that he had done an impressive job in outlining how he wanted to act.

Questions

1. What self-guides or actions were important to Mr. Reilly as a new teacher?

2. What self-guides or actions were important to Tim before the start of class?

3. What self-guides became important to Tim after Mr. Reilly spoke?

4. Are Mr. Reilly's and Tim's self-guides detailed enough to help them see whether they are acting in the ways they want to act?

Use the student's answers to highlight the following key points:

► Self-guides include ideal ways of acting, as well as ways one should not act.

► Self-guides need to be detailed.

► Self-guides allow you to make corrections by helping you see whether your actions match the way you want to act or believe you ought to act.

7.2 Creating a Self-Guide

Ask the student to think of a time when she could have been better at doing what she ought to do or should do, according to her teacher and parents (for example, doing her homework, participating in class, working harder to pay attention). Ask the student to picture in detail an alternative way she could act in the situation—a way that would make her feel proud of herself and show others that she is doing what she is supposed to do.

To help her be able to act in this hoped-for way, ask the student to pretend that she is preparing a movie script that she will use to act in this alternative, positive way. Tell the student that to prepare for her role in the movie, she needs to be aware of the many physical elements of the scene in which the action will occur (such as in study hall or a classroom); the "characters" who will participate in the scene (the teacher, other students); the exact, detailed actions that she, the star, will perform and not perform; and the order in which she will carry out the actions. Ask the student to create a name that reflects how she wishes the character to be (for example, Sally Super-Conscientious, Rhonda Responsible, The Calm and Careful One).

Work with the student to rehearse the script, trying to anticipate any challenges that might arise as she imagines herself performing the positive behavior. Together, problem-solve ways to overcome any of the challenges.

Encourage the student to imitate her make-believe performance in a real-life situation during the coming week. Discuss some ways that she could remember the acting guidelines, including what she did in the past that helped her keep something important in mind. Ask her to keep track of how close she came to matching the part so that she can discuss it during the next session.

At the next session, if she reports that things did not go as planned, ask her to try to figure out why. Was she truly motivated to act the way she had planned? Did she put forth enough effort? Ask the following questions as well:

1. Did the way you act fit your character's name?

2. Did your actions "fit together" and made up a sensible, whole character?

3. Were you able to keep in mind the way you wanted to act? If so, how did you do it?

4. Did your parents or teachers comment about any of the behaviors you were trying to demonstrate this past week? If so:

   a. Did their comments focus on what you did that they were impressed by or proud of, or did their comments focus on how well you met your obligations?

   b. Did their comments make you think that they have the same opinions as you do about desirable ways of acting?

   c. Did their comments affect how you felt about acting in the desired ways?

   Use the student's answers to emphasize the following:

   ► The value of having a clear and detailed image to use in establishing and following positive guidelines

   ► The importance of considering ideals, "shoulds," and "oughts"

   ► The value of mental rehearsal

   ► The need to keep guidelines relevant and appropriate

   ► The importance of monitoring the match between guidelines and actual behavior and correcting any discrepancies

   ► The effects of teacher and parent comments on following guidelines

7.3 Clarifying the Nature of a Possible Self

Explain to the student that it is helpful to imagine how he would like to be and not be in the future. He can do this by thinking about someone he knows or a famous person. Tell the student that imagining his anticipated or "possible self"—how he would like to be—will help him plan, problem-solve, and rehearse, and will likely help him become the type of person he really wants to be. By rehearsing, the student will be able to consider the specific steps that he needs to take to reach his goals, the order that the steps should be placed in, and the ways that the present and future are connected. As a result, the student is likely to feel more confident about accomplishing the goals, and he will have a path or road map for monitoring his progress.

To help make clear the nature of a possible self, tell the student you are going to read or have him read the following story and will ask him to answer several questions about it.

Stacy

Stacy was upset. This was the third time she had gotten in trouble for being late in the past two weeks. Stacy imagined what her mother would say to her after her mother got the call from the school: "You don't think about anything other than yourself. You never follow the rules. You just do what you feel like and what is easy. If you keep this up, you are never going to accomplish anything." Maybe her mother was right. Stacy usually did do what she felt like—and didn't think much about the future. It probably was time to try to get her act together.

She thought of the people she admired and immediately pictured Grandpa Phil. He had grown up really poor, quit school, and took a job to help his family pay their bills. He then went into the navy, and, when he got out, he finished his high school diploma while he worked as a television repairman. When he was 50 years old, he saw an ad looking for men in the "trades" who wanted to be trained as vocational teachers. They would then be offered jobs at the local high school and help young people, who were poor like he had been, learn a trade and get a job. He took the training and taught for 15 years. He once showed her a scrapbook with a bunch of thank-you letters from his students, and, from what she read, he seemed to have been a great teacher—someone who really cared about the kids and went out of his way to help them.

Questions

1. What does Stacy admire about her grandfather?
2. Do you think Grandpa Phil is a good model of a person you would *like* to be?
3. Do you think Grandpa Phil is a good model of a person you think you *should* or *ought* to be?
4. If Stacy were to follow in Grandpa Phil's footsteps, where should she start?
5. How might Stacy tell whether she was making progress in being like Grandpa Phil?

Highlight the following key points when discussing the student's responses:

► The importance of imagining something in the future that is valued

► The need to consider both what seems ideal and what seems required

► The need to consider short-term as well as long-term steps in a journey

► The need for specific strategies to achieve the next set of steps

7.4 Creating a Possible Self (Part 1)

Ask the student to select and describe a celebrity, such as a famous athlete, politician, movie star, historical figure, or singer she admires. Then ask the following questions:

1. In as much detail as possible, what seems attractive about the person?

2. In what ways do you think you are currently like and not like this person?

3. What would you have to do and not do to be more like this person in the future?

4. What steps do you imagine that the person has taken to become the way he or she is now (for example, did the person go to a special school or study under a great coach)?

5. Do you feel you are capable of being similar to this person in the future? If not, do you feel you could become more similar to this person with learning, effort, and/or assistance?

Use the student's answers to highlight these key points:

➤ The value of having an aspiration

➤ The need to use past accomplishments to gauge expectations

➤ The importance of confidence

7.5 Creating a Possible Self (Part 2)

Ask the student to imagine himself one year from now. Ask him to describe the image in as much detail as possible, including what in particular would make him feel proud of himself and what he would have to do—and not do—to be the way that he imagines (that is, what are his "oughts" and "shoulds"). Tell the student that before he answers, you are going to share the responses of two other students to this question, to help him think about his own responses.

Student A

Next year, I don't want anyone to notice that I have an attention disorder. I would be proud of myself if I could focus, listen when the teacher is talking, not say things quickly without thinking first, and not get into trouble because I talk too much during class. I should make sure to take my ADHD medicine. I want to become aware of when I am ready to say something, and then take a minute to think before I talk. Also, I should make lists of the things I need to do and make sure I check them.

Student B

In a year, I want to get the Study Skills Champion Certificate and show my mom that I am making an effort to do better. Last year, the principal gave out a list of study skills and said he would honor students who demonstrated these skills throughout the year by giving them a special certificate. I should start my work ahead of time, remember to bring home the books I need to do my homework, start my homework each day at the same time, keep track of when I have to hand in things, check directions really carefully, and make sure my folders and book bag are organized.

Ask the student to describe his image of how he would like to be in a year. Tell him to include the steps he will need to take and also to note the things he should not do in order to be the way he hopes to be next year. Ask the student to focus especially on what his first step would be and how he will try to carry out this first step.

When the student has finished, summarize what he said about his future image and ask these questions:

1. On a scale of 1 to 10, how important to you is being the possible self you imagined next year?

2. On a scale of 1 to 10, how confident are you that you will act like this possible self next year?

Use the student's ratings to emphasize the following key points:

► Motivation strongly influences effort.

► Confidence strongly influences a person's effort and willingness to persist in the face of a setback.

Focusing on the first step in the student's plan, ask:

1. Is the strategy that you picked to get to your first step realistic, and is it something that you can do and are willing to do?

2. Is there anyone that you can check with to get an opinion as to whether your strategy is a good one?

3. How can you keep track to see whether you are using your strategy in the way you intended?

4. If you successfully carry out your strategy and complete the first step in your journey toward your possible self, how do you think you will feel?

5. If you fail to carry out your strategy and complete the first step, how do you think you will feel?

Now tell the student that in order to be the way he wants to be in a year, it is helpful to create a "road map" or path that starts where he is now and indicates the steps that he needs to take to arrive at the point where he is acting like the possible self he wants to be.

Tell the student that you are going to use the two examples you presented earlier to illustrate what you mean.

► *Student A:* For the first step toward his goal, the student who imagined himself as not being noticed for having an attention disorder picked taking his medication as prescribed for one month. His second step was to think before talking, and he decided he would try to do that for an entire week.

► *Student B:* As her first step toward achieving her possible self, the student who wanted to be a Study Skills Champion next year decided to make sure that her folders and book bag stayed organized for one month. As the next step, she decided to finish her homework on time for one month.

Ask the student to keep his possible self in mind and describe one or two steps he could take toward becoming that person. Use his answers to emphasize that imagining a future possible self is valuable for these reasons:

► It allows for mental rehearsal.

► It helps clarify and enhance attention to priorities and relevant actions.

► It connects actions and thoughts.

► It underlines the need for strategies.

► It makes a future goal seem more attainable.

8

Self-Monitoring

OVERVIEW

Self-monitoring is the process of observing the degree of match between a student's actual behavior relative to academic goals and the standards he has set. The interventions in this chapter focus on enhancing the degree of self-awareness and ability to manage attention to permit self-monitoring of performance.

The Importance of Awareness and Self-Observation

To successfully regulate academic behavior, students need to be aware of, and systematically observe, their actions so that they can keep their goals in mind; assess whether their behavior is in accord with their goals, standards, and pre-selected strategies; and gauge their progress. Awareness and self-observation are especially critical elements of academic self-regulation. Students must be able to notice discrepancies between their actions and how they desire to act—and use this information to make any necessary corrections. Thus, for students to be academically self-regulated, they need to be aware of their future goals and the standards that they have set in the present to represent these future desired behaviors; attend to these behaviors; note "errors" or discrepancies when they occur; make any necessary self-corrections; and put forth effort to stay on the path toward their desired academic goals (Carver & Scheier, 1982).

The ability to be aware—to be conscious of either an internal state or an external event—is primarily determined by a person's ability to allocate and manage attention. Because there is usually more information present than the brain can process, students need to prioritize the types of information that they consider relevant and attend selectively—that is, direct their attention to the relatively small amount of information that is relevant to accomplishing their goals. Next, they need to maintain a vigilant state and direct their focus on this information as they work at achieving their goals (Allport, 1989; Reid, 1996). Academic self-regulation is thus enhanced when students are able to increase the attention-drawing power of their academic goals, standards, and strategies and are able to block distracting information that interferes with their focus on desired behavior (Posner & Petersen, 1990).

Attention Management

The ability to voluntarily employ attention in order to stay focused on goals and resist distractions varies widely among young people. These differences in attention management are evident from the beginning of life. Youth differ in the length of time that they take to orient to a stimulus and in their capacity to sustain attention, due in part to early differences in ability to experience interest in an object. Thus, by the end of their first year, children differ in their ability to sustain attention in the face of distractions (Rothbart & Jones, 1998). By around age 4, they differ in their ability to pay attention to aspects of the environment that are relevant to carrying out a task and ignore irrelevant stimuli (Ruff & Rothbart, 1996).

Because attention is multidimensional, youth are likely to differ in their strengths and weaknesses in regard to attention management (Derryberry & Reed, 2002). Differences are frequently found in ability to selectively engage attention and focus on the relevant "target characteristics" of a task; to disengage attention from a task, shift attention, and flexibly engage attention on another task; to divide attention among tasks; to be vigilant, sustain attention, and maintain a particular focus over a period of time; to detect errors; and to inhibit or block responses that may distract them from sustaining their focus (Posner & Petersen, 1990; Ruff & Rothbart, 1996).

Students who pre-plan, that is, anticipate the goals that they want to achieve, the standards that they will use, and the strategies that they will enact, are more likely to be academically self-regulated. Students who have a detailed mental representation of their intended actions, know the cues that they will use as reminders, and establish a time and place to perform a task are more likely to engage their attention on the specific aspects of academic situations that relate to attainment their goals. They are also more likely to retrieve the pertinent information, sustain their attention, and resist distractions (Gollwitzer, 1999).

A student is especially likely to find mental rehearsal or pre-planning helpful in managing attention if his pre-plan includes detailed strategies, such as the use of self-talk, to focus on relevant aspects of his plan; "tunnel vision" to narrow attention and help resist the pull of irrelevant cues; and environmental restructuring to remove novel or potentially distracting stimuli (Gollwitzer, 1999). Paradoxically, distractions such as background noise can at times facilitate attention management. The energy required to ignore distractions such as background noise can increase the amount of effort that a student expends to maintain focus on relevant cues, thus engaging him more fully in the task (Ruff & Rothbart, 1996).

The Importance of Language in Attention Management and Self-Monitoring

Language competence, particularly competence in using private speech (speech directed to oneself), is a critical ingredient of attention management. Thus, the use of such statements as "What's my goal in this situation? I need to concentrate and stay on task" and "Am I acting the way I should act?" strongly facilitates a student's ability to control and direct her attention (Meichenbaum, 1977). Self-directed language enhances attention management in several specific ways: First, the use of private speech can increase the distinctiveness of relevant internal and external cues and make the elements of a task—and the student's goals—more salient. Second, private speech provides the student with a guide to help direct her focus while working on a task. Third, private speech helps the student be aware of information that she has stored in memory. Fourth, private speech helps inhibit the urge to focus on information that competes with a task and the student's goals. Finally, private speech can enhance the student's focus on the match between her actual behavior and performance standards, thereby facilitating the use of self-correcting behavior (Meichenbaum, 1977; Vygotsky, 1962).

Self-Monitoring and Academic Self-Regulation

In the context of academic self-regulation, self-monitoring has two essential functions: It increases the student's awareness of his desired academic target behaviors and provides feedback on the degree of congruence between what he had hoped to do or felt he ought to do and what he is actually doing. Developmentally, youth can monitor their performance as early as preschool—for example, being able to tell whether a block tower they have built is identical to a model they are trying to copy. Starting at around age 3, children show noticeable improvements in self-monitoring or error detection, seemingly as a result of their improved ability to solve problems (Jones, Rothbart, & Posner, 2003).

Students are more likely to use self-monitoring when they choose a goal rather than when the goal is imposed (Zelazo et al., 1997), consistent with the finding that motivation increases when students select their own academic achievements (Deci & Ryan, 1985). In addition, self-monitoring is more likely to be effective in motivating students to match their actual and desired behaviors when they focus on a small set of target behaviors attached to clear, specific standards (Baumeister, Heatherton, & Tice, 1994). Self-monitoring is also more likely to enhance academic self-regulation when students follow a systematic, detailed plan that includes a recording method (diaries, progress worksheets) and contains specific information about the time, place, and duration self-monitoring should occur. Finally, self-monitoring is more likely to be effective when it is enacted regularly, is performed in proximity to the event to be monitored (Zimmerman, 1989a, 1989b), and includes external prompts to signal the need to self-monitor (Shapiro & Cole, 1999).

A recording method is an especially valuable part of self-monitoring. By recording observations about the degree of match between actual and desired behavior, the student is likely to feel increased responsibility for the outcome she is trying to achieve and to remain focused on the desired standard and the degree of correspondence between actual behavior and the standard she is trying to maintain (Reid, 1996).

Self-monitoring recording methods that are particularly effective often contain the following elements: carefully defined objective criteria, preset times the recording will be made, and a specific definition of what will be recorded. In addition, effective recording methods tend to include self-assessment standards that help the student decide whether her behavior matches the "reference value," or target behavior, and a planning section so that if there is a discrepancy, the student can identify actions she could take to better meet the desired standard in the future (Shapiro & Cole, 1999). Empirically, the effectiveness of formal self-monitoring procedures in academic settings varies depending on what is being monitored. Although self-monitoring procedures have been found to dramatically increase on-task behavior for all ages and instructional settings, these procedures have produced equivocal effects on academic productivity and have an unclear effect on accuracy, typically measured when a student is working on academic tasks (Reid, 1996).

INTERVENTIONS

8.1   Highlighting the Nature of Self-Awareness and Self-Observation (Part 1)

Explain to the student that in order to tell whether she is acting in agreement with the goals, standards, and pre-planned strategies that she has set, she needs to be self-observing—that is, vigilant while performing academic tasks and aware of whether her actions correspond to the behaviors that she wishes to demonstrate.

If the student notices that she is not keeping to the plan she has set, she can use this information to make self-corrections and get back on track. Emphasize that being aware of one's thoughts, feelings, and actions is critically important in maintaining standards and in achieving academic goals.

Tell the student that to help her practice being self-aware, you are going to ask her to perform two mental exercises. First, ask the student to imagine that she has been selected to recite the Pledge of Allegiance and should do so slowly and clearly, while standing erect. Next, ask her to imagine that she is standing on the stage in the school auditorium and facing the entire student body while saying the words of the pledge.

Tell the student that you are now going to ask her to actually stand, place her right hand over her heart, imagine that she is on the school stage, and say the words of the pledge aloud. You will first tell her the words of the pledge and then ask her to follow the instructions you have given. Say: "I pledge allegiance to the flag of the United States of America, and to the Republic for which it stands: One nation under God, indivisible, with Liberty and Justice for all."

Now ask the student to say the pledge while imagining the scenario described. Give reminders as needed.

When she is finished, ask her whether she did the following:

1. Tried to remember the instructions while reciting the pledge. If so, what did she say to herself to help do so?

2. Felt calm, nervous, or neutral.

3. Felt that she was following the instructions perfectly. How could she tell (for example, said it slowly and clearly, stood erect)?

4. Was distracted. If so, what happened?

Summarize the student's self-observations and compliment her ability, where possible, to note both internal data (thoughts, feelings) and external data (distractions).

8.2 Highlighting the Nature of Self-Awareness and Self-Observation (Part 2)

For the second exercise, tell the student that you are going to ask her to do a brief writing task. You are not going to read what she writes. Instead, you are going to ask questions about what she thought and felt while she was writing.

First, ask her to think of a favorite television show that she watches a lot. Next, ask her to imagine that she is entering a contest in which she will pick a favorite episode, change one thing (small or big) about it, and try to make the change as interesting and imaginative as possible. In this contest, the writer who makes the most interesting and creative change in an episode will win and get to spend a whole day with the show's stars.

Hand the student a blank sheet of paper and a pencil and remind her to begin by thinking of a particular episode, change one thing about it, and try to make the change as interesting and creative as possible. Ask her to begin writing. After five minutes, stop her and ask these questions:

1. Were you interested and involved in the writing exercise?
2. Were you able to concentrate?
3. Did you think you did a good job?
4. Did you follow the instructions?

Use the student's responses to inquire about the "mental data" that she used to answer the questions, and highlight that being self-observing involves noticing how one thinks, feels, and acts, as well as how various aspects of a situation affect her.

8.3 Illustrating the Importance of Preplanning in Directing Attention to Goals and Standards

Explain to the student that being self-observing when trying to reach a goal is more likely to occur if he has prepared a plan that includes, in great detail, both the specific actions he will perform and the order in which he will perform them. By previsualizing the plan and keeping it in mind while performing, the student will be able to observe whether he is doing what he has pre-planned. Tell the student it is also helpful to visualize being successful—doing so has been shown to increase a person's confidence.

Ask the student to pick an upcoming academic task. Work with him to develop an appropriate short-term goal for that task. For example, he might want to be very accurate in his work, stay on task, and try the hardest he can. Together, picture ways he would need to act and not act to achieve the goal, and arrange the mental images into a sequentially organized, visual narrative using the analogy of creating a movie script. As part of his picture, ask the student to include a description of the setting, the time the task is to be done, the important, specific actions to be taken, and any possible events that might interfere.

Then ask the student to observe, when he actually performs the task, how closely his actions match his plan—particularly any occasions when his behavior matched the plan really well and any occasion when his behavior did not match the plan. In regard to the latter, ask the student what he did when he noticed there was a mismatch.

8.4 Recognizing the Importance of Concrete Markers in Self-Observation

Work with the student to develop an image of a desired "possible self" that she could try to be like in the coming week, along with an image of a possible self she would not like to be. Help her create as detailed and vivid an image as possible of these desirable and undesirable ways of acting.

Next, highlight the "concrete markers," or specific behaviors, the student could use to gauge whether she is acting in the way she wants and avoiding acting the way she does not want to act. Explain that she will be more likely to tell whether she is keeping to her plan if she focuses on the specific actions she needs to observe. For example, if she desires to be a careful worker as a possible self, she could focus on making sure she has the materials needed for homework before she leaves school, reviews what she needs to do before the homework is started, begins her homework on time, and checks to be sure that she completes all the assignments and does them accurately.

Restate the value of being specific when checking one's progress in sticking to a plan. Tell the student that being specific will allow her to obtain feedback to help her know in detail what she needs to do to reduce any mismatches between her current actions and the desired standard.

Together with the student, identify an academic goal that will require a fair amount of self-control to achieve (for example, to hand in her homework on time). Help her visualize the goal in as specific and concrete a way as possible, and then ask her to take theses steps:

1. Rate the value and/or importance of the goal on a 0 to 10 scale.

2. List the benefits and costs that she anticipates if she achieves the goal.

3. Develop a "scientific" way to judge whether, during the next week, she is meeting these performance indicators (for example, each night she will check against her planner that all work has been done, put the completed work in her book bag, and hand the work in the next day).

Work with the student to enter the behaviors to be monitored on a **Behavior Recording Sheet,** as well as the time and place she will record whether she has demonstrated the planned behaviors (see Figure 14). Make sure that the student uses objective criteria, establishes a time and place to

FIGURE 14   Behavior Recording Sheet

Behavior	Criteria	Match (Y/N)	Day/time checked

From *Self-Regulated Learning: Practical Strategies for Struggling Teens*, by Norman Brier, © 2010, Champaign, IL: Research Press (www.researchpress.com, 800-519-2707) record her progress, includes a specific definition of what she will record, and has a concrete way to judge whether she has met the reference standard.

Ask the student to try during the coming week to demonstrate the behaviors she has identified. Ask whether she anticipates any problems in filling out the recording sheet, and, if so, work with her on ways to overcome these problems.

Finally, ask the student to review her completed recording sheet before your next meeting and think about whether she used the concrete markers to determine whether her behavior matched her standards. If it did, ask her how it felt—specifically, whether her behavior was effective in helping her reach her goal. If it did not, ask her how that felt and what she thinks she can learn from the recording sheet to help her make progress in the future.

8.5   Finding Ways to Maintain Self-Monitoring

Explain to the student that self-monitoring, or checking the degree of match between her behavior and the academic goals and standards that she has set, is most helpful if she monitors herself regularly. To self-monitor on a regular schedule, reminders or prompts are particularly helpful. Explain that setting up a way of regularly reminding herself to check whether she is acting in the way she desires will help her keep the desired behavior in mind, and, if necessary, bring her attention back to the desired behavior if she loses focus on these behaviors.

Ask the student to think about the following example.

Sam

Sam has set the goal of staying on task in math. He will measure his goal by checking periodically during his math class to see whether he feels interested and is paying careful attention to what the teacher is discussing—and is not thinking about things that have nothing to do with the class.

Work with the student to identify ways that Sam can remember to check whether he is acting in the way he hopes to, highlighting the distinction between informal, nonsystematic ways of checking and systematic procedures such as using a watch that can be set to beep or a cell phone that can be set to vibrate at regular intervals. Ask the student to think of other possible ways that Sam could get a reminder signal. For example, when doing schoolwork at home he could make a tape recording of his own voice saying at random times on the tape such phrases as "Are you paying attention?" or "Hey, you—focus!"

Remind the student about her previously selected academic goal that required a fair amount of self-control, and help her visualize that goal in a specific, concrete way. Then help her select an external prompt that she could use to remind herself to self-monitor between now and the next meeting. Explain that when the prompt occurs, she should focus, visualize the desired behavior, and consider whether she is acting in the way she has planned.

Explain that a prompting or reminder system should include how often prompts occur. Work with the student to determine an appropriate interval between reminders and whether the reminders should be at set times or random times. Once the plan is finalized, review how the Behavior Recording Sheet is to be filled out, particularly the last column (day/time checked).

Before ending the discussion, ask the student whether she feels confident about her level of motivation to follow the plan. If the answer is no, ask her whether she thinks a reward would help her feel more motivated. Explain to the student that honesty about one's motivation is important in achieving the desired behavior.

One way of increasing motivation is to draw up a contract. As an example of this approach, the student might put some money (the amount of which would be negotiated) in an envelope, or ask her parents to do so. At pre-established times, the student (or her parents, if they are the "bankers") would determine, based on her recording sheet, whether she had kept to the contract. If so, she could withdraw the money as a self-reward.

Ask the student whether she thinks self-rewards are a good idea to help her make sure she is keeping track of what she needs to do. If she feels that a contract would be helpful, draw up the contract with her, and ask the student to discuss the idea with her parents. If they agree, implement the plan for the contracted period of time. Decisions to continue or discontinue the contract are based on whether the reward system seems to be helping the student work at monitoring and achieving her desired behavior.

8.6   Improving the Ability to Pay Attention

Explain to the student that the ability to pay attention is especially important when trying to follow a plan. It is necessary to identify the important information that relates to the plan, attend to this information, and, if interrupted, bring attention back to this goal-relevant information. At times, the student will have to divide his attention between two or more tasks, pay attention for a relatively long time, and not let himself be distracted.

Tell the student that to find out what help he needs in managing his attention, you are going to ask him to read a series of statements from the **Managing Attention Questionnaire** (Figure 15). He is to respond to each statement by indicating whether he thinks it is never true, sometimes true, often true, or always true.

Based on the student's answers, provide feedback about whether he may need to work extra hard to focus on relevancies, sustain attention, resist distractions, re-engage attention, and/or divide his attention between important tasks.

FIGURE 15 Managing Attention Questionnaire

Read each statement and then decide whether it is never true, sometimes true, often true, or always true for you.

	Almost never true	Sometimes true	Almost always true	Always true
1. I can concentrate on my schoolwork.	❑	❑	❑	❑
2. I can concentrate on my schoolwork when I am in a noisy situation.	❑	❑	❑	❑
3. I become distracted when I try to do my schoolwork.	❑	❑	❑	❑
4. I can switch back and forth between two things that I have to do and still pay attention to both.	❑	❑	❑	❑
5. I can quickly find important pieces of information when I do my school work.	❑	❑	❑	❑
6. I do not pay attention to distracting thoughts while I work.	❑	❑	❑	❑
7. I feel involved when I am doing my schoolwork and concentrate.	❑	❑	❑	❑
8. I can pay attention for the whole time that I am working.	❑	❑	❑	❑
9. I can return my attention to my school-work after if I am interrupted and stay focused on it.	❑	❑	❑	❑
10. I can go back and forth between paying attention to what the teacher is saying and to the information in the book that the teacher is asking us questions about.	❑	❑	❑	❑

From *Self-Regulated Learning: Practical Strategies for Struggling Teens,* by Norman Brier, © 2010, Champaign, IL: Research Press (www.researchpress.com, 800-519-2707)

8.7　**Demonstrating How to Manage Attention Better**

Explain to the student that there are strategies she can use that might improve her ability to focus on and follow a plan. These strategies include arranging the work environment to help her focus; minimizing potential distractions; talking to herself about what needs to be attended to while working; and gently but firmly moving her attention back to a task when unrelated thoughts come to mind, while resisting the urge to concentrate on these unrelated thoughts.

Ask the student to make a plan for the coming week about how she would like to act while doing a school task. Help her picture how she would need to act and not act to achieve this goal, and suggest how she might organize the plan as a sequential, visual narrative, using a movie script as an analogy. Her movie script should include a description of the setting, the time the actions are to occur, and the specific actions that need to be taken. Also discuss anything that could occur that would interfere with the plan, and together think about how these interferences might be dealt with.

Suggest that the student use the following ideas to try to be the best manager of attention that she can be. Here are some ideas she can try:

1. Post a list of what she should do, and in what order, in a spot that she is likely to look at often, such as a mirror in her bedroom or a bulletin board.

2. Make sure that her materials (papers, books, pencils) are neat and organized.

3. Keep in her workspace only the materials for the task she is currently working on.

4. Eliminate or reduce distractions.

5. Use a reminder system to see whether she is keeping to the script.

Tell the student you will check next time to see how good an attention manger she was able to be.

8.8　**Using Meditation to Help Focus Attention**

Explain to the student that meditation is one way to improve attention management and the ability to keep to a plan. When the student feels he is having a hard time concentrating, he can try to "anchor" his focus on his breathing to calm down and center his attention. He should also note distractions when they occur—but not react or focus on them. Instead, he should gently move his attention back to his breathing anchor.

Tell the student that you are going to coach him in using meditation. Ask him to sit in a relaxed, upright position, put all of his thoughts aside, and concentrate on his breathing. Tell the student to carefully observe how the air is moving in and out of his body, how his stomach rises and falls, how the air enters his nose and leaves his mouth, and how each breath changes and is different from the breath that came before. Ask the student to try to be aware of when his attention wanders, and, at these times, to note the distraction rather than try to ignore it or push it away. Advise the student not to react to the distraction but to calmly and gently move his attention back to his breathing anchor.

Now ask the student to practice anchoring his attention on his breathing for three minutes. Tell him you will let him know when the three minutes is up. When the exercise is completed, review the results and praise any successes the student has demonstrated in mastering the technique.

Tell the student that together you are going to try an experiment. In a little while, you will ask him to imagine what the last day of the school year will be like. While the student is imagining this scene, ask him to remain alert and to notice whether his mind wanders. If it does, explain that he should make note of it, without judgment or reaction, and try to gently bring his attention back to his breathing and then to the scene he is imagining.

Ask the student to pick one occasion in the coming week where it is important that he keep to a plan and to try to "catch" himself when his mind wanders, focus on his breathing at such times for about a minute, and then return his focus to his plan. Explain that at the next meeting, you will ask how he did.

8.9   Highlighting the Value of Self-Talk

Explain to the student that *self-talk*—saying particular statements to herself—can help her be self-observing and better manage her attention. Explain that talking to herself (in her mind, not out loud) will help her be more aware of important information in a situation; remember what she needs to do and how she wants to act and not act; feel in control by providing guidelines or directions to follow; judge how she is doing; and notice errors and discrepancies between how she is acting and how she wants to act.

Select a plan that the student has made earlier and explain that particular statements can be used to help stick to a plan at different points in time. Tell the student that you are going to offer some statements that she can say to herself when she is getting ready to start a plan, while she is carrying out the plan, and afterward, when reviewing how she did. Review or provide a copy of the **Helpful Self-Talk** handout (Figure 16).

FIGURE 16   **Helpful Self-Talk**

When getting ready, it is helpful to say to yourself:

► What is my plan?

► What do I need to focus on?

► Where should I start, and what are the steps that I should follow to keep to my plan?

While working on the plan, it is helpful to say to yourself:

► Am I keeping to my plan?

► Am I doing things the way that I wish to do in order to feel proud of myself?

► Am I focusing on the particular ways I want to act?

Afterward, it is helpful to say to yourself:

► Did I keep to my plan?

► What did I do that I feel proud of?

► What can I do differently to make progress?

From *Self-Regulated Learning: Practical Strategies for Struggling Teens,* by Norman Brier, © 2010, Champaign, IL: Research Press (www.researchpress.com, 800-519-2707)

The Role of Mood

9

OVERVIEW

A student's ability to act in an academically self-regulated manner is strongly affected by his mood or relatively enduring emotional state (Gendolla & Brinkman, 2005). Mood affects the ability to be academically self-regulated by influencing action preferences, the ability to manage attention and process information, and the capacity to mobilize and direct effort. More specifically, a student's mood affects academic self-regulation by determining how rewarding and interesting he finds a task to be, the perceived difficulty of the task, the degree of confidence he experiences while performing it, the estimation of effort that seems necessary to complete the task successfully, and the point at which he desires to stop expending effort (Ashby et al., 1999; Blair, 2002; Campos, Frankel, & Camras, 2004; Gendolla & Brinkman, 2005).

Positive and Negative Mood

When in a positive mood, students are more likely to be open to new academic experiences; be in a state of interested engagement; be optimistic, confident, and able to notice positives in themselves and their academic experiences; expend effort; and be capable of experiencing academic tasks as pleasurable and satisfying. In contrast, students in a negative mood are more likely to be disengaged, self-doubting, and aware of deficits in their performance and in the academic experience. They are also more likely to be unwilling to expend effort and be displeased while engaging in an academic task. As a result, academic tasks are more likely to be perceived as requiring more effort than the student is willing to expend—and thus the student is less likely to attempt the task (Ashby et al., 1999; Campos, Frankel, & Camras, 2004; Gendolla & Brinkman, 2005).

Mood has a particularly strong effect on attention management. When students are in a negative mood, especially if they are prone to over-arousal, they are likely to attend to the source of their distress rather than to the relevant information that needs to be learned (Derryberry & Reed, 2002). In addition, once distressed, they are likely to remain preoccupied with their distress and have significant difficulty in transferring their attention back to school tasks (Brand, Reimer, & Opwis, 2007; Spurr & Stopa, 2002).

Specific Effects of Mood on Academic Self-Regulation

A depressed mood has an especially powerful negative effect on academic self-regulation. Students who display such symptoms as persistent sadness, irritability, self-criticalness, disinterest, fatigue, and hopelessness are unlikely to feel self-efficacious when performing academic tasks. In addition, they are less likely to view school as important or relevant compared to their current state of distress, set academic goals, attend to school tasks, expend effort when in school, and expect to succeed (Cole, 1991; Roeser, Eccles, & Someroff, 1998; Schwartz et al., 2005; Sideridis, 2005;).

When a student is depressed, her belief that she can influence people and events to produce a desired outcome is negatively affected, and thus she is less likely to believe that she can personally influence academic outcomes and experience academic success (Bandura, 1997). Students who do not feel self-efficacious tend to be passive and fail to assert their needs when at school. In addition, they tend not to initiate actions to complete school tasks, use poor problem-solving strategies while working, and, if successful, tend to view their academic successes as a result of external causes, such as luck, rather than as a result of their own efforts (Nolen-Hoeksema, Girgus, & Seligman, 1986). These negative outcomes are enhanced when the student attributes her lack of academic success to a personal deficit that is permanent and global, such as, being "born stupid" (Bandura et al., 1999).

One especially frequent cause of a depressed mood in school-aged children is peer rejection and social isolation while at school (Farrer & Skinner, 2003). Students who are rejected by peers tend to have a negative social self-image and feel highly self-conscious, sad, and lonely. When at school, they tend to be withdrawn and disengaged learners, and they have a great deal of difficulty focusing on their schoolwork. They also are likely to be less trusting, anticipate little support from others, and, overall, view school as a negative experience (Buhs, Ladd, & Herald, 2006; Flook, Repetti, & Ullman, 2005; Ladd, Kochenderfer, & Coleman, 1997; Wentzel, 1999).

INTERVENTIONS

9.1 Assessing Mood

Explain to the student that how he feels when at school or doing homework affects how much he wants to try to learn, how much effort he will put forth, how well he can pay attention, how confident he will be, and how much interest he will have in what is being taught. Tell the student that in order to gain information about his typical mood when doing schoolwork, you are going to ask him to answer a series of questions from the **Assessing Mood Questionnaire** (Figure 17) about how he felt this past month. For each question, he should tell you how often he felt that way: never, sometimes, often, or almost always.

Review the student's responses with him, and decide whether he seems prone to being in a bad mood while at school or doing homework. If so, explain that you will suggest some things that he can do to maintain a positive attitude.

9.2 Staying Positive

Explain to the student that what he focuses on has a lot to do with whether he will be in a positive or negative mood. People are more likely to feel positive when they believe that what they are doing is pleasurable and that they can be successful at the task.

Review with the student the details of a school occasion when it was important that he do well, then say that you would like to challenge him. The challenge is that he has to list as many positive things as he can about what he did well on that occasion and what was pleasurable or satisfying about the experience. Explain that to do well on the challenge, he has to mention things that most students would feel proud of or good about—the things he describes do not have to be extraordinary. Develop the list with the student, helping him identify as many positives as he can, including, if possible, enjoyment while learning and improvement at the task.

Ask the student to review his school experiences each night for the next week before going to bed. He is to write down in a notebook selected just for this purpose any positives that he noticed that day in regard either to his academic performance or to the school day. Suggest that the student use the following phrases to do the assignment:

► "Today I felt good about myself for_____."
► "Today I liked _____ at school."

At the next meeting, review the student's notes and ask whether he felt that focusing on what he did well and enjoyed helped him stay positive.

FIGURE 17   Assessing Mood Questionnaire

Check the option that best describes how often you have experienced any of these moods and feelings during the past month.

During the past month when at school or when doing homework, I have felt . . .	Never	Sometimes	Often	Almost always
1. Sad	❑	❑	❑	❑
2. Hopeless	❑	❑	❑	❑
3. Unable to concentrate	❑	❑	❑	❑
4. No pleasure while doing schoolwork	❑	❑	❑	❑
5. Lonely	❑	❑	❑	❑
6. No interest in schoolwork	❑	❑	❑	❑
7. Tired	❑	❑	❑	❑
8. Self-critical	❑	❑	❑	❑
9. Helpless	❑	❑	❑	❑
10. Irritable	❑	❑	❑	❑

From *Self-Regulated Learning: Practical Strategies for Struggling Teens,* by Norman Brier, © 2010, Champaign, IL: Research Press (www.researchpress.com, 800-519-2707)

9.3   **Disengaging from Negative Thoughts**

Explain to the student that one way to avoid being stuck in a negative mood is not to think about an upsetting thought over and over again (for example, "I am no good at this" or "I never will be able to finish this in time"). Students who feel negative have a great deal of difficulty focusing on their schoolwork. Instead, their minds usually go back to what made them upset. Even when students are able to attend to something besides the upsetting thought, they often wind up thinking about the upsetting thing again after a short time.

Explain that one way to stay positive and not keep thinking about upsetting things is to use meditation. Meditation is composed of two parts: One part is focusing on the "anchor" of one's breathing, and the other part is noticing negative thoughts that come to mind and not reacting or thinking further about them. Instead, the student gently moves his attention back to the anchor of his breathing. If appropriate, remind the student that this technique of meditation was suggested earlier as a way to help stay focused (intervention 8.8).

Tell the student that you are now going to coach him in using meditation. Explain that meditation will help him feel that there is a space between him and his negative thoughts and that using this technique can help him feel that he has the power to prevent negative thoughts from continuing to be upsetting.

- ► First, ask the student to sit in a relaxed, upright position. Tell him that the practice time for this exercise is three minutes and that you'll let him know when the time is up.

- ► Second, tell him to try to put all of his thoughts aside and concentrate on his breathing.

- ► Third, tell him to carefully observe the way air is moving in and out of his body, how his stomach rises and falls, how the air enters his nose and leaves his mouth, and how each breath changes and is different.

- ► Last, tell the student that when he becomes aware that his attention has wandered, he should note the thought rather than try to ignore it or push it away, and then, without thinking further about the thought, calmly and gently move his attention back to the anchor of his breathing.

When the practice is complete, review the results, praising whenever possible what he did well. Ask the student to practice meditating anytime during the coming week when he notices that he is having repetitive negative thoughts.

9.4   Challenging Feelings of Helplessness

Explain that a person can get in a bad mood when she feels defeated and believes there is no way that she can do what is being asked. This belief about being defeated is often wrong, however. Frequently, it is possible to make things better if we can find ways of figuring out the problem, examine whether we have the facts right, and think of alternative strategies to try, including seeking help.

To practice ways the student can challenge feelings of helplessness and try to improve a school situation, ask her to think of a time when she was asked to do something at school and felt that she could not do it. Ask the student to explain why she felt incapable or helpless. Then, work together to challenge the facts.

Ask the student whether she could have done any of the following:

1. Tried harder
2. Used a different strategy
3. Asked for help
4. Revised her goal
5. Modified her standard of success
6. Changed the situation (for example, asked for extra time; asked for permission to delay taking the test)

As part of the discussion, ask the student whether she felt that she was:

1. Being too self-critical
2. Failing to notice what she was doing right
3. Failing to notice any positive feedback

Use her responses to highlight the importance of these key points:

► Being active, not passive, when facing a challenge
► Thinking of things you can do, especially changing strategies and asking for help
► Being aware of what you can do right and the positive aspects of the situation

9.5   Overcoming Feelings of Not Being Liked

Explain that one frequent reason students get in a bad mood at school is that they feel other students dislike them or do not want to include them in activities. When students have these feelings of rejection, they often become self-critical, sad, and lonely; have trouble focusing on their schoolwork; and do not like being at school.

Tell the student that you are going to ask him a series of questions from the **Assessing Feelings of Not Being Liked** handout (Figure 18) about whether he feels rejected or excluded at times. Explain that you want him to think about this past month when answering. For each question, he should tell you how often he felt that way: never, sometimes, often, or almost always.

Review the student's responses with him and determine whether he seemed to feel rejected or excluded while at school. If so, explain that you can suggest some things he can do that might help.

9.6 Coping with Feelings of Being Teased or Left Out

If the student responds to the series of questions in ways that suggest that he feels rejected or excluded by peers, ask him to describe, in as much detail as possible, examples of specific occasions that illustrate the problem. Help the student to be as complete as possible in describing each occasion, using a narrative framework: Ask him to tell you how each episode began, what happened next, and how the episode ended. Also ask the student to describe how he thought, felt, and acted at each point in the narrative sequence.

After the student describes the examples, repeat back to him your impression of the main ideas he presented (for example, "Kids really give you a hard time about your weight" or "Jimmy seems to get everyone to pick on you"). Focus on ideas that are recurrent, and describe how you think the student seems to feel ("I see how sad you feel when you describe being teased"). Ask the student to correct anything you said that he feels is inaccurate.

Explain to the student that it is easy, when upset, not to see or hear things accurately, especially the intentions of others. Together with the student, review the episodes again to see whether he misperceived social information. Where possible, consider alternative explanations to his perceptions (for example, "I know you think Jane ignored you—do you think she might have been distracted or was just feeling quiet?").

Explain that when people feel threatened, they tend to overfocus on what they think is the source of the threat and ignore alternative, positive social information. Ask the student to look back and think about whether there might have been a peer or adult who was present, or aware of the occurrence, who had tried to be kind or supportive during or after the upsetting episodes. If so, ask the student how he responded to these supportive attempts and how he might respond in the future to get the most benefit from this person's support.

Ask the student to be a "scientist" this coming week and objectively study situations to see whether, in fact, other students intend to be hurtful or exclude him. If the student thinks that the facts support that others are being hurtful or excluding him, ask him to try to notice whether there is a "trigger," or specific cause, that starts the hurtful behavior (for example, "Jimmy makes a joke about my weight and then the other kids join in" or "I blurt out my thoughts and then everyone laughs at me").

FIGURE 18   Assessing Feelings of Not Being Liked

Check the option that best describes how often you have experienced any of these thoughts or feelings during the past month.

During the past month at school, I have felt . . .	Never	Sometimes	Often	Almost always
1. Left out by other students	❏	❏	❏	❏
2. Threatened by other students	❏	❏	❏	❏
3. Separate or apart from other students	❏	❏	❏	❏
4. Lonely when at school	❏	❏	❏	❏
5. Picked on by other students	❏	❏	❏	❏
6. Teased by other students	❏	❏	❏	❏
7. Unsupported when upset by other students	❏	❏	❏	❏
8. Withdrawn	❏	❏	❏	❏
9. Taken advantage of by other students	❏	❏	❏	❏
10. Talked about by other students	❏	❏	❏	❏

From *Self-Regulated Learning: Practical Strategies for Struggling Teens,* by Norman Brier, © 2010, Champaign, IL: Research Press (www.researchpress.com, 800-519-2707)

As part of encouraging the student to be objective, ask him to try to be aware of whether he is failing to notice positive social information. Specifically, ask him to try to find a smiling, friendly face, or a student who sends a welcoming, inclusive, positive message when he is in a situation where he expects to be teased or left out. If the student can identify positive information, ask him to try to remember how the smile or positive message made him feel.

Explain to the student that, as mentioned, many different strategies can be used to improve a situation. Work with him to identify a particular problem or problems that have resulted in his being rejected or excluded, then identify some strategies that he can use. For example, the student might try to identify a classmate who seems friendly or who shares a special interest and initiate an attempt to spend time with him.

1. Label, or assign words to, the problem(s) identified. For example, the student states, after a discussion, "I get very quiet when I feel they are laughing at me, and then I feel lonely."
2. Brainstorm alternatives to improve or eliminate the problem(s).
3. Decide which alternative seems best.
4. Plan and, if necessary, practice the alternative by visualizing it.
5. Try the alternative.
6. Afterward, evaluate whether the alternative was helpful.
7. Make any modifications if needed, and try again.

It might be necessary to provide an additional, more intense level of intervention to improve the student's social situation. If so, work with the student and his family to arrange it.

Controlling Anxiety

OVERVIEW

The ability to focus on academic goals is often undermined by anxiety. When students are excessively worried, nervous, fearful, and/or self-conscious, they are likely to divide their attention between task-relevant thoughts and their anxiety-linked thoughts. As a result, they are less likely to focus their attention on the pertinent aspects of the learning task and have difficulty encoding, storing, organizing, retrieving, and remembering task-relevant information (Sarason, 1972). They also have difficulty absorbing information, monitoring their performance, and flexibly shifting from one strategy to another (Kuhn, 1999).

Anxiety interferes with academic self-regulation, in part, by increasing the likelihood that a student will be perceptually and cognitively oversensitive to aspects of academic situations that seem related to the possibility of failure and, as a result, will lose motivation to achieve academic goals (Lewis, 1992). When anxious, students tend to anticipate failure, fear embarrassment when performing an academic task, avoid performing the task, or begin work but fail to persist. They also tend to avoid asking for help, fearing they will experience shame, embarrassment, or humiliation if they do (Covington, 1992; Flook, Repetti, & Ullman, 2005).

Procrastination

Anxiety is often expressed in the form of procrastination. Students who fear academic failure often delay or defer engaging in an academic task that needs to be completed—for example, not handing in school assignments, handing them in late, cramming, or not preparing sufficiently (Wolters, 2003). Students who procrastinate often fail to act conscientiously (Costa & McCrae, 1992). They tend to see themselves as weak or lazy, do not work methodically, lack persistence, and are poor at time management. In addition, they tend not to feel self-efficacious, are poor at tolerating frustration and discomfort, and have deficient impulse control. Finally, students who procrastinate are often aware that negative consequences are likely to result from their avoidant behavior (Schraw, Wadkins, & Olafson, 2007; Steel, 2007).

The likelihood that a student will procrastinate and avoid working toward academic goals is affected by the interval between the time a school task is assigned and the time it needs to be completed and the degree to which the student anticipates that the academic task will be aversive (Steel, 2007). The more time the student is given to complete an assignment, and the more the rewards for completing the task are perceived as being distant in time, the greater the likelihood that the student will procrastinate. Similarly, students who anticipate that an academic task will be aversive are more likely to procrastinate when asked to perform the task (Howell et al., 2006; Steel, 2007).

Perfectionism

Perfectionism is also a frequent contributor to anxiety in academic settings. Students who display perfectionism tend to set standards that they cannot realistically achieve. While trying to achieve their academic goals, students who display perfectionism are likely to worry excessively about making mistakes, be indecisive, ruminate about possible errors, overscrutinize what they do, and postpone or avoid doing their work, fearing that they will fail to meet the standards that they have set (Bieling et al., 2003; Shafran & Mansell, 2001).

INTERVENTIONS

10.1   Being Aware of Anxiety When Doing Schoolwork

Explain to the student that when she is anxious, it is likely that it will be harder to focus on schoolwork, remember what needs to be learned, and track what she is supposed to do. Explain that there are many causes of anxiety. For example, some students worry that they will do poorly on a test and feel anxious that they will be punished for not doing well, while others worry when confused about how to do their schoolwork and anticipate that the teacher will be critical of them for not understanding the material.

To determine how anxious the student is when doing schoolwork, tell her that you are going to ask a series of questions from the **Schoolwork Anxiety Questionnaire** (Figure 19) about how she has felt when doing schoolwork this past month.

Review the student's responses with her to determine whether she seems overly anxious while doing schoolwork. If so, explain that you can suggest some things that she can do to feel less anxious and can work together to determine whether a more formal treatment for anxiety might be needed.

10.2   Understanding the Effects of Anxiety

Explain that when someone is nervous, tense, and/or scared, he tends to have a harder time paying attention, in part because he is likely to be distracted by how his body feels. When nervous, a person will experience physical reactions such as sweating, breathing more rapidly, and having feelings of tightness in his muscles. A person is also likely to become preoccupied with thoughts related to the issue that is making him nervous. For example, if a student is worried about doing badly on a test, he will think a great deal about the test, and it will be harder for him to pay attention to what he needs to learn.

Have the student think of times when he was nervous at school or when doing homework. Ask him to describe how he felt at those times and to make his descriptions as complete as possible. To help the student elaborate, he can be asked, "Did you feel preoccupied? Distracted? Restless? Tense?" "Did you have an upset stomach, tense muscles, rapid breathing, or a headache?" and so on. Encourage the student to comment specifically on the ways that these body reactions, feelings, and thoughts affected his ability to do schoolwork.

Next, ask the student to think of himself as a scientist and to objectively examine his level of anxiety when doing schoolwork. Give him a copy of the **My Anxiety Signals** handout (Figure 20). Explain to him that anxiety signals are made up of feelings, behaviors, and body reactions. Review the anxiety signals in each of the categories on the handout and make sure the student understands them.

FIGURE 19   Schoolwork Anxiety Questionnaire

Check the option that best describes how often you have experienced any of these feelings or physical reactions during the past month when you think about your schoolwork.

How often did you . . .	Never	Sometimes	Often	Almost always
1. Have dizzy feelings, nauseous feelings, and/or trouble catching your breath?	❏	❏	❏	❏
2. Have trouble remembering what you needed to do for school?	❏	❏	❏	❏
3. Check and double-check your schoolwork?	❏	❏	❏	❏
4. Have difficulty making decisions?	❏	❏	❏	❏
5. Have trouble concentrating?	❏	❏	❏	❏
6. Feel nervous, shaky, or tense?	❏	❏	❏	❏
7. Feel scared all of a sudden for no reason?	❏	❏	❏	❏
8. Feel restless?	❏	❏	❏	❏
9. Have thoughts or pictures that kept coming to your mind?	❏	❏	❏	❏
10. Feel worried about being embarrassed or humiliated?	❏	❏	❏	❏

From *Self-Regulated Learning: Practical Strategies for Struggling Teens,* by Norman Brier, © 2010, Champaign, IL: Research Press (www.researchpress.com, 800-519-2707)

FIGURE 20 **My Anxiety Signals**

For the next five days of the school week, place a check mark in the box to indicate any of these anxiety signals that you experienced.

Feelings	Day 1	Day 2	Day 3	Day 4	Day 5
1. Overwhelmed	❑	❑	❑	❑	❑
2. Fearful, nervous, tense	❑	❑	❑	❑	❑
3. Irritable	❑	❑	❑	❑	❑
4. Uncomfortable, ill at ease	❑	❑	❑	❑	❑
5. Tired	❑	❑	❑	❑	❑
6. Unable to remembering things	❑	❑	❑	❑	❑
7. Unable to concentrate	❑	❑	❑	❑	❑

Behaviors					
1. Can't stay still	❑	❑	❑	❑	❑
2. Jumpy	❑	❑	❑	❑	❑
3. Eat too much or too little	❑	❑	❑	❑	❑
4. Forgetful	❑	❑	❑	❑	❑
5. Very quiet	❑	❑	❑	❑	❑

Body Reactions					
1. Tight muscles	❑	❑	❑	❑	❑
2. Ache in head or stomach	❑	❑	❑	❑	❑
3. Pounding heart	❑	❑	❑	❑	❑
4. Rapid breathing	❑	❑	❑	❑	❑
5. Sweaty	❑	❑	❑	❑	❑
6. Faint/dizzy	❑	❑	❑	❑	❑
7. Nauseated	❑	❑	❑	❑	❑

From *Self-Regulated Learning: Practical Strategies for Struggling Teens,* by Norman Brier, © 2010, Champaign, IL: Research Press (www.researchpress.com, 800-519-2707)

Ask the student to place a check mark next to any anxiety signals that he experiences while doing schoolwork each day during the coming school week. Tell him that you will discuss his "data" at your next session. During that discussion, try to identify triggers that set off the student's anxiety (for example, he expects his parents will be mad if he doesn't do well, the assignment was given by a particular teacher, he has to speak in front of the class). Explain that you will offer some suggestions to help reduce anxiety.

10.3 Strategies for Coping with Anxiety

Students can learn to cope with nervous feelings and prevent anxiety from interfering with their ability to achieve academic goals and plans by becoming skilled in these areas:

1. Recognizing their anxiety signals

2. Identifying the potential causes of their anxiety

3. Noting the specific ways in which their anxiety interferes with their ability to learn

Explain to the student that simply knowing more about a problem and its causes often can reduce anxiety. Better understanding provides a greater sense of control and increased hope that solutions to reduce anxiety can be identified. Point out to the student that it is particularly helpful to talk about one's nervous feelings with a trusted person. Other people, at times, can be more objective about fears and can help clarify the facts in a feared situation, as well as identify strategies to lessen anxiety.

Tell the student that certain strategies are especially helpful to reduce nervous feelings that interfere with achieving school goals. Three strategies are particularly effective:

1. Relaxation techniques

2. Meditation to manage attention

3. Problem-solving techniques

Explain that you are going to describe each of these strategies in detail and help the student learn how to apply them. A key part of putting the strategies to use is being alert to anxiety signals. Coping strategies are most effective when the anxiety level is relatively low. Therefore, the student needs to practice recognizing her anxiety signals when they first arise. She can then select and implement one or more of the three strategies as soon as possible.

10.4 Using Relaxation Techniques to Reduce Anxiety

Explain that relaxation techniques help lessen or eliminate nervous feelings and bring about a sense of calmness. Remind the student that the best time to use these techniques is either when she first notices an anxiety signal or before an event that predictably has made her nervous in the past (for example, before a test, speaking in front of the whole class). Explain that it is important to practice the techniques so that she can use them effectively when they are needed. Also explain that some techniques will be more effective for her than others. Therefore, the student needs to experiment and see which techniques work best for her in reducing anxiety.

Explain, demonstrate, and then have the student demonstrate each of the following relaxation techniques. Give her feedback and have her continue practicing the techniques until she seems proficient.

Muscle Relaxation

Ask the student to tense and then relax her hands, and, while she is doing so, ask her to carefully pay attention to the change in sensation from being tense to being relaxed. Next, ask the student to hold her fist as tight as she can for about 15 seconds and then slowly spell out the word *tense* (saying one letter every two seconds). Then ask her to relax her hand quickly and slowly spell the word *relax*. Explain to the student that she can repeat this technique as needed until she feels calmer.

Deep Breathing

Ask the student to watch as you demonstrate a deep, regular, diaphragmatic breath. While doing so, highlight and demonstrate the difference between deep breathing and tense, uneven, rapid breathing. Show the student how to take a deep breath through her nose, hold her breath, and slowly and evenly exhale through her mouth. Explain to the student that she should try to breathe as naturally as possible, slowly filling her lungs with air and then slowly emptying her lungs.

Counting

A simple but effective relaxation technique is counting. Ask the student to silently count backward from 20 to 0, at a slow and even pace. Explain that this technique is even more effective in reducing anxiety if she combines counting backward with the deep breathing technique. Ask the student to give this combination a try, counting backward from 20 to 0, while taking a diaphragmatic breath between each number.

When the student seems proficient in using each of the relaxation techniques, ask her to try applying them in the coming week, either when she is about to enter a learning situation that almost always makes her anxious, or when she notices an anxiety signal while doing schoolwork.

Ask the student to try to determine which technique works best at calming her down in which particular learning situation. Tell her that you will ask about her experiences in using these techniques next time and will check to be sure that she is using them in the most effective manner.

10.5 Using Meditation to Manage Attention When Anxious

If appropriate, remind the student that meditation was suggested earlier as a way to help him stay focused and disengage from negative thoughts (interventions 8.8 and 9.3). Meditation is also an effective technique to stop worries that interfere with one's ability to pay attention while doing schoolwork. Meditation is particularly helpful in resisting a focus on something that is making the student nervous or on thoughts that are preoccupying him.

Tell the student that you are now going to coach him in meditation.

► First, ask him to sit in a relaxed, upright position, try to put all of his thoughts aside, and concentrate on his breathing.

► Next, ask the student to carefully observe how the air is moving in and out of his body, how his stomach rises and falls, how the air enters his nose and leaves his mouth, and how each breath changes and is different from the breath that came before.

► Now ask the student to practice "anchoring" his attention on his breathing for three minutes; you will tell him when the three minutes is up.

When the practice is complete, review the results, provide corrective feedback as needed, and praise any successes the student has demonstrated while practicing.

Ask the student to try to notice during the coming week when his attention wanders away from his schoolwork—toward either the "threat" in the situation or to his preoccupations—and then do as follows:

1. Note the source of anxiety rather than try to ignore it or push it away.
2. Use meditation.
3. Without focusing on the threat or preoccupation, try to calmly and gently move his attention back to his breathing anchor and then to the school task.

Tell the student that, at the next meeting, you will ask how well the technique worked and whether he has any questions about its use.

10.6 Using Problem-Solving Techniques to Reduce Anxiety

Explain to the student that knowing what makes her anxious and when she is anxious is an important step in figuring out a plan to be less anxious. Tell the student that you are going to teach her some ways to problem-solve and better define what the problem is—and what she can do to make things better.

Explain that the first step in problem solving is putting the problem into words—that is, answering the question, "Why am I anxious?" For example, if the student feels anxious before a test, the problem might be that she is scared of failing; if she is anxious when called on in class, the problem may be that she is worried about sounding dumb and feeling embarrassed.

The second step in problem solving is to brainstorm and think of all the different strategies the student can use to reduce or eliminate the problem so that she can be less anxious. The student might ask herself, "What can I do to be less anxious?" (for example, ask for help, discuss my concern with my parent, try harder) and "What has worked in the past?" Tell the student that it is especially helpful, when anxious, to try to be objective and compare the facts with her worries to see whether her concerns are realistic or excessive (for example, did she actually fail the test? Was she actually laughed at by other students?). Explain that, at times, our worries are not consistent with the facts and that when she carefully examines the situation—and corrects any misperceptions—her anxiety is likely to decrease.

Explain to the student that once the list of alternative strategies is complete, the third step in problem solving is to imagine trying the alternatives and considering the likely pros and cons that would result—that is, "What is good or bad about each strategy? What might go right and wrong?" The student then weighs those pros and the cons and decides which strategy seems to be the best by asking herself, "When I consider all the strategies, which is likely to help me be less anxious?"

The final step in problem solving is to implement one of the strategies and evaluate its effectiveness in reducing anxiety. Ask the student to imagine a situation in which she is likely to be anxious about a school goal in the next week. Together, go through each of the problem-solving steps of describing the problem, brainstorming various strategies, considering the pros and cons of each, and selecting the best. Next, rehearse the strategy and plan for its actual implementation. Tell the student that after giving the strategy a try, she should evaluate how the plan went and ask herself, "Did the plan work?" and "What can I do better next time?"

Tell the student that when you meet next time, you will discuss the results and see how the plan may be improved or revised.

10.7 Identifying and Challenging Avoidance

Explain that when students anticipate being anxious, they are likely to intentionally delay or postpone doing their schoolwork. They may hand in their work late or not at all, or rush at the last minute and hand in a poor product because they did not have enough time to do the work. Tell the student that you are going to review a series of questions from the **Identifying and Challenging Avoidance** handout (Figure 21) to see how much he has avoided or put off his schoolwork this past month.

FIGURE 21   Identifying and Challenging Avoidance

Read the statements in the list below. Place a check mark in the box to indicate how often you did any of these things in the past month.

	Never	Sometimes	Often	Almost always
1. Put off doing schoolwork	☐	☐	☐	☐
2. Completed schoolwork by the time it was due	☐	☐	☐	☐
3. Intended to start schoolwork right away and hand it in on time	☐	☐	☐	☐
4. Judged correctly the amount of time needed to complete the schoolwork	☐	☐	☐	☐
5. Avoided doing work that was unpleasant to do	☐	☐	☐	☐
6. Avoided doing work that couldn't be done very well	☐	☐	☐	☐
7. Avoided doing work that you thought might be criticized	☐	☐	☐	☐
8. Picked something enjoyable to do instead of completing schoolwork	☐	☐	☐	☐
9. Did schoolwork just before it had to be handed in	☐	☐	☐	☐
10. Had to rush to finish schoolwork to get it in on time	☐	☐	☐	☐

From *Self-Regulated Learning: Practical Strategies for Struggling Teens,* by Norman Brier, © 2010, Champaign, IL: Research Press (www.researchpress.com, 800-519-2707)

Together, review the student's responses and decide whether avoidance of schoolwork is a problem. If it is, try to determine whether anxiety about doing the work (as opposed to a lack of motivation) contributes to the avoidance. If anxiety is a big contributor to avoidance, ask the student whether he would like to use a problem-solving or relaxation technique to change this behavior. If so, coach him in those techniques.

10.8 Dealing with Procrastination

Explain that one form of avoidance is *procrastination*—putting off something that has to be done to a later time. Procrastination is especially likely when there is a lot of time between when a school task is assigned and is due, as well as when the school task is considered to be unpleasant or is anxiety provoking.

Ask the student whether she has recently procrastinated (that is, put off doing an assignment until just before it was due). If so, work with the student on the first step of problem-solving and attempt to figure out the nature of the problem. Next, ask the student:

1. On a scale of 0 (not at all important) to 10 (very, very important), how important is it to you to reduce procrastination?

2. On a scale of 0 (no confidence at all) to 10 (very, very confident), how successful do you think you will be in controlling your urge to procrastinate?

If the student considers reducing procrastination important, even if she is not very confident about her ability to do so, explain that planning is an important way of overcoming procrastination. Writing down what, when, where, and how work will be done, and keeping track of the plan, will help increase the student's sense of control, which, in turn, will help her procrastinate less. If the student does not consider reducing procrastination important, tell her if at a later point she decides it is, you can help her try to change.

Ask the student to describe an upcoming assignment that does not need to be handed in for at least one week. If possible, she should pick an assignment that she thinks she will likely do at the last minute or hand in late. Together, develop as many reasons as possible about why it is important for her to do the school task and to plan the specific steps that need to be carried out in order for her to complete the assignment on time and without waiting until the last minute. Make sure to include in the plan, when, where, and how the work will be done. Also make sure that large tasks are broken down into their component parts.

Next, have the student make a schedule to determine whether she has done what she intended to do (for example, every night at 9 P.M., she will note on the schedule whether she worked when, where, and how she intended).

Ask the student to make checking her compliance a routine or habit— something she does automatically, without thought. Also suggest setting short-term goals, or indicators of progress, to provide concrete and timely evidence that she is being successful. Point out that if she "messes up" and procrastinates, she should try to notice why, then problem-solve and try to get back on track as soon as possible.

Tell the student you will review the results of her attempt to overcome procrastination at the next meeting.

10.9 Challenging Excessive Perfectionism

Explain that many students feel anxious and worry that they will not do well enough because the standard that they use to judge their performance is too high (for example, a student compares himself to peers who receive the best grades on a test or to peers who are on the honor roll). When a student's standards are too high, he is more likely to become preoccupied and anxious about doing well, and, as a result, is less likely to do well and more likely to avoid doing his schoolwork.

Ask the student whether he has trouble setting a fair or reasonable standard for judging how he is doing in regard to schoolwork. To help determine whether he is setting excessive standards, ask him to describe a recent time where he wanted to do really well at something in school but was unable to follow through with his goal. Then ask the following questions:

1. Can you think of any reasons why you did not do as well as you had hoped?

2. Do you think that failing to achieve the standard means that you have a flaw or defect?

3. Do you think that the standard you set may have been too inflexible or unrealistic—for example, did you have to read ten chapters in just two days?

4. Was your standard inconsistent with your prior achievements?

Using the example the student identified, help him understand what might have been a reasonable standard, based on his past performance, circumstances, and level of effort.

Next, ask the student to select an upcoming school task. Work with him to establish a reasonable and realistic standard that he can use to judge his performance. Ask him to use this new standard to judge his performance on the upcoming task and to notice whether using the standard helps him feel better about his performance (that is, whether it helped him feel less anxious and less avoidant).

11

The Social and Physical Context

OVERVIEW

Academic self-regulation is strongly influenced by the nature of a student's social interactions and physical context. Academic self-regulation is relatively high when caregivers (such as parents, guardians, and other important adults) encourage autonomy, display interest, provide support, convey acceptance, and maintain high expectations for academic success. Academic self-regulation is also higher when caregivers modulate their own emotional reactions to students' academic behavior and allow them to express negative emotions. Academic self-regulation, in addition, is higher when students are allowed to carry out their schoolwork as autonomously as possible, in a structured and predictable environment. In such an environment, guidelines, assistance, strategies, and corrective feedback are provided when needed, and routines are used to help direct action and organize knowledge. Finally, academic self-regulation is higher when a student's peers possess values that support school success and when they model behavior that makes school success more likely.

Caring and Academic Self-Regulation

Students who feel cared about and emotionally connected to their caregivers feel more secure. They are likely to feel worthy of love and believe that they are capable of being considered special and important by others (Connell & Wellborn, 1991). A student's sense of being cared about is influenced, in large part, by the degree to which his caregivers are actively involved in his activities. Thus, when caregivers take time to interact with the student, show affection,

121

and are attuned to his emotions, the student shows higher levels of engagement when working on academic tasks and higher levels of energy, effort, enthusiasm, self-reliance, and persistence (Farrer & Skinner, 2003; Gonzales DeHass, Willems, & Doan Holbein, 2005). The student is also more likely to perceive his caregivers as sensitive and accessible, be more trusting, and believe that support will be available when needed (Bowlby, 1979). As a result, students who feel cared about are likely to display higher levels of curiosity and exploration in learning situations and are more likely to avail themselves of support when faced with an academic challenge (Deci, Ryan, & Williams, 1996). Conversely, students who feel that their caregivers are uninvolved and unresponsive are likely to demonstrate greater difficulty in becoming engaged when presented with school tasks and are more likely to experience anxiety and frustration while working (Farrer & Skinner, 2003).

Internalization of Caregiver Values

Students who view their caregivers as warm, interested, and accepting are more willing to comply with caregiver directives and internalize their caregivers' goals, values, and standards in regard to academic achievement. Conversely, students who view their caregivers as displaying high levels of negative emotions in regard to their school performance, and who feel that their caregivers are not concerned about their interests, are less motivated to comply with their caregivers' directives and are less motivated to adopt caregiver standards in regard to academic behavior (Eisenberg et al., 2001).

Caregiver expectations have a particularly strongly effect on a student's perception of what she considers to be desirable academic goals and standards of success (Nurmi, 1991). The strength of the effect is determined, in large part, by the clarity, frequency, and directness of these types of caregiver communications (Higgins, 1991; Wentzel & Wigfield, 1998); the degree to which caregiver messages are harmonious with the student's values, goals, and standards (Dix, 1991); and the extent to which caregivers consider the student's perspective when the student is presenting her point of view. Students are more likely to incorporate their caregivers' values when caregivers allow them to make choices, negotiate value differences, and seek and accept compromises (Deci, Ryan, & Williams, 1996).

Caregiver support for student autonomy is an especially powerful determinant of whether the student will work toward academic goals that her caregiver has endorsed. When a caregiver appreciates the student's feelings and perspective and supports her ability to make autonomous choices, the student is likely to have more opportunities to practice self-regulation and see the connection among her actions, personal academic goals, and values (Connell & Wellborn, 1991). As a result, she is likely to be intrinsically motivated and persistent in achieving goals (Deci, Ryan, & Williams, 1996). In contrast, when a caregiver is controlling and uses such techniques as love withdrawal and guilt induction when the student is not acting in ways that the caregiver feels she ought to, the student tends to have less opportunity to experience and internalize strategies of academic self-regulation (Kochanska, Tjebkes, & Forman, 1998).

Reflected Appraisals

A student's sense of academic competence and aspirations are strongly affected by the reflected appraisals of individuals in her social context, who become a "looking glass" for her (Cooley, 1902). Caregiver messages about the likelihood that the student will be successful when attempting academic tasks, in particular, strongly affect the student's sense of self-efficacy and beliefs about whether she is in control of the means to be successful when attempting to achieve a desired academic outcome. Clear, consistent, and explicit messages by caregivers that the student is viewed as competent are associated with a student's having higher expectations for academic success and with higher levels of effort, engagement, and persistence while working on academic tasks (Skinner, 1991).

Reflected appraisals, or reactions to mistakes and failures, have an especially strong effect on academic self-regulation. When caregivers react to mistakes and failures by withdrawing affection or inducing guilt, students are more likely to avoid academic tasks, be fearful about the possibility of failure, and be overconcerned about the quality of their performance (Elliot & Thrash, 2004). These negative effects on performance are particularly likely if caregivers are insensitive to the student's feelings and wishes and disregard her point of view at these times (Soenens et al., 2005).

Affective Regulation in Caregivers

Caregivers' ability to regulate their own emotional reactions affects students' ability to maintain self-control when engaged in academic tasks. Students are more likely to persevere, complete their schoolwork, and appropriately regulate their emotions when caregivers are calm, positive, empathic, and supportive. On the other hand, students are less willing to do their schoolwork and regulate their emotions when caregivers have difficulty regulating their own emotions and are negative, irritated, or impatient (Pomerantz, Wang, & Ng, 2005).

A positive attitude and a relatively low level of emotional arousal by caregivers facilitate academic self-regulation by allowing students to better manage their attention, process information, inhibit behavior, and plan (Eisenberg et al., 2001). Academic self-regulation is also facilitated when caregivers use warmth and encouragement to allow the student to express negative feelings. When a student's negative feelings are encouraged rather than suppressed, his negative emotions are likely to become less intense. Therefore, he is more likely to hear the caregiver's messages accurately and respond flexibly and in an organized manner (Baumrind, 1971).

The Effects of Feedback and Assistance

Given the important role that feedback and the availability of guidelines play in academic self-regulation, the degree of assistance and structure that is present in a student's environment are critically important. Students display higher levels of academic self-regulation as the amount and quality of knowledge and assistance available to them increases. However, because autonomy and self-reliance are also essential elements of academic self-regulation, assistance is more likely to facilitate academic self-regulation when it is offered after the student experiences an impasse in learning and thus sees the assistance as necessary and valuable. Academic self-regulation is lower when unsolicited help is repeatedly offered (Grolnick, Ryan, & Deci, 1991), in part because students tend to view unsolicited help as an indication that their caregivers believe that they have low ability, and, as a result, they feel that they are being viewed negatively (Graham & Barker, 1990). Even when a student requests assistance, academic self-regulation is more likely to be enhanced if caregivers offer the least amount of support possible that still allows the student to perform the academic task successfully and if the support is nonevaluative, includes corrective feedback, and provides positive social reinforcement for effort and persistence (Corno, 1989; Wood, Bruner, & Ross, 1976).

The specific nature of the evaluative feedback given by caregivers while providing assistance also affects a student's sense of academic competence and intrinsic motivation. When caregivers provide positive feedback in a noncontrolling manner, students have relatively high levels of efficacy and intrinsic motivation. On the other hand, when caregivers provide negative feedback in a critical and controlling manner, students often display low levels of efficacy and intrinsic motivation (Deci, Ryan, & Williams, 1996). In addition, when caregivers display sympathy following poor academic performance, or praise success on easy tasks, the student is more likely to infer that she has low ability, is more likely to expect to fail, and will often lose motivation. Similarly, when caregivers display anger and criticism following poor academic performance, the student is more likely to infer that she has failed to make sufficient effort and to believe that she is unable to meet the caregiver's expectations for higher performance (Graham & Barker, 1990).

The Role of Peers

Peers with whom the student regularly interacts, and especially those who are perceived as close friends and similar to the student, strongly influence his level of academic self-regulation (Oyserman & Terry, 2006; Ryan, 2001). The effect of peer influence on academic self-regulation becomes stronger as students get older, most likely because, with age, they are more likely to spend greater amounts of time with peers compared to parents and other adults. Peer influences are especially strong in early adolescence, when the need to conform to the peer group and to compare oneself to other group members is relatively high (Altermatt & Pomerantz, 2003; Steinberg & Silverberg, 1986).

Peers can influence academic self-regulation in several ways. Students tend to associate with peers who share similar academic beliefs and behaviors—that is, who have similar grade-point averages, academic aspirations, homework habits, and levels of engagement in schoolwork (Ryan, 2001). As a result, they are more likely to be motivated to match or model these academic beliefs and behaviors as they exchange academic experiences and information, and thus tend to develop even more similar levels of effort, standards, strategies, and aspirations in regard to academic pursuits (Oyserman & Terry, 2006). For example, the likelihood that a student will have a high standard of acceptable academic behavior and little tolerance for engaging in a choice that departs from this standard is strongly affected by the degree to which her peers participate in class and study for tests.

Peer pressure in regard to specific academic beliefs and behaviors is often conveyed through direct feedback, indirect feedback in the form of gossip, and inclusion and exclusion from participation in peer activities (Gest et al., 2008). Thus, peers seem to provide a comparative standard that students use to mentally rank and judge their academic performance and competence (Butler, 1998).

With regard to the effects of peers on specific elements of academic self-regulation, peer associations significantly affect the level of intrinsic value a student places on school and the amount of enjoyment experienced when involved in school activities (Ryan, 2001); expectations for success and sense of academic competence; the nature of the explanations the student develops to explain good or poor performance (Altermatt & Pomerantz, 2003; Gest et al., 2008; Ryan, 2001); and the level of engagement while carrying out learning activities (Kinderman, 1993). However, there is only a modest relationship between peer influence and a student's academic standards and aspirations. The somewhat weaker nature of this relationship is most likely due to the significant influence that caregivers have on a student's academic standards and aspirations (Altermatt & Pomerantz, 2003; Ryan, 2001).

The Importance of Structure and Predictability

Academic self-regulation is higher when the home environment is organized, distraction free, and consistent, particularly if information, feedback, and strategies to achieve desired academic outcomes are provided when needed. Within such an environment, students are more likely to enact strategies and maintain academic standards, especially if they also establish and follow routines.

Routine activities allow a student to carry out academic tasks more quickly and effortlessly, in part because having a routine increases the likelihood that the student will be on "automatic pilot" and not dwell on the question "Do I want to do this?" In addition, when students follow routines, they are likely to feel, and to be, autonomous, given the reduced need for supervision and prompting by others.

The use of routines, however, brings the risk that the student will be less aware of his actions while enacting a task, and, as a consequence, will be less attentive to details (Logan, 1988). Routines are more likely to positively affect academic self-regulation when the student problem-solves, and, based on past challenges when trying to achieve academic goals, participates in designing the routine to minimize any negative effects —for example, dealing with the past challenge of handing his homework in on time by employing the routine of starting work at the same time and place each school day (Brier, 2006; Perry, 1998).

INTERVENTIONS

11.1   Assessing the Caregiving Context

Explain to the student that her ability to achieve academic goals depends a lot on the degree to which she feels cared about and supported by important people in her life. Tell the student that to better understand how she feels in this regard, you are going to review a series of statements from the **Assessing the Caregiver Context** handout (Figure 22) and have her answer, based on her experiences in the past month, whether she strongly agrees, agrees, disagrees, or strongly disagrees with each statement.

Summarize the student's answers, highlighting key themes (for example, "My parents are good listeners and let me say how I feel" or "My parents are not the 'touchy, feely' type and are more interested in what I do wrong than what I do right").

11.2   Improving the Level of Caring and Acceptance by Caregivers

If the student's responses to the questionnaire suggest that he feels that his caregivers are insufficiently caring, interested, attuned, or helpful in regard to academic achievement, inquire whether he would like to brainstorm ways to improve the situation.

Explain that there are at least three ways that he might try to make the situation better:

1. With planning and practice, he could discuss his concerns with caregivers and do his part to help make things better.

2. You could meet with his caregivers, at least initially, and act as a spokesperson for the student so that they could better understand his concerns and determine whether a meeting would be helpful.

3. He could meet with a person trained in helping families get along better.

If the student wants to take the lead and see whether he can discuss ways of making things better with his caregivers, ask him to imagine how he might express what he feels and to visualize, in as much detail as possible, how he expects his caregivers to react. Critique the student's ideas and work together to identify the strategy that seems best.

Next, rehearse the strategy, using modeling and role-playing. In the rehearsal, determine the best time and location for the discussion and the best words to use, as well as the best ways to say them. Ask the student to try the plan, and, if he reports that the results are somewhat positive, coach him about how he can continue to improve the situation. If the results are not positive, discuss whether a joint meeting might be helpful or whether consulting a family expert might be a good idea.

FIGURE 22   Assessing the Caregiving Context

Read the statements in the list below. Place a check mark in the box to indicate whether you strongly agree, agree, disagree, or strongly disagree with each.

	Strongly agree	Agree	Disagree	Strongly disagree
1. My parents allow me to choose how and when I do my schoolwork.	❑	❑	❑	❑
2. My parents are affectionate.	❑	❑	❑	❑
3. My parents are interested in what and how I do at school.	❑	❑	❑	❑
4. My parents tell me clearly and frequently that they expect me to do very well at school.	❑	❑	❑	❑
5. My parents tell me clearly and frequently why they think school is important.	❑	❑	❑	❑
6. My parents try to help me with schoolwork when I need help.	❑	❑	❑	❑
7. My parents do not criticize my schoolwork if I try my best.	❑	❑	❑	❑
8. My parents stay calm when I don't do well at school.	❑	❑	❑	❑
9. My parents do not get angry when I make a mistake at school.	❑	❑	❑	❑
10. My parents do not try to make me feel guilty or scared when I make a mistake or fail.	❑	❑	❑	❑
11. My parents let me express my frustrations and angry feelings about school.	❑	❑	❑	❑
12. My parents are understanding and listen to my point of view about school.	❑	❑	❑	❑
13. My parents compliment me when I do well at school.	❑	❑	❑	❑
14. My parents expect me to be successful at school.	❑	❑	❑	❑
15. My parents tell me what they think about my schoolwork without making me feel bad.	❑	❑	❑	❑

From *Self-Regulated Learning: Practical Strategies for Struggling Teens,* by Norman Brier, © 2010, Champaign, IL: Research Press (www.researchpress.com, 800-519-2707)

If the student has asked you to be a spokesperson, review what you intend to say to his caregivers so that he can confirm that you are accurately reflecting his views. Have the meeting, review the results with the student, and then plan an appropriate follow-up (for example, having a joint meeting, consulting a family expert). If the student plans to takes part in any follow-up meeting, help him practice how he might act to make meeting as successful as possible. Highlight the importance of the student's demonstrating that he is able to compromise, listen, empathize, and take the perspective of others, as well as take personal responsibility for the outcomes of his choices.

11.3 Getting Support from a Helpful Adult

Ask the student whether she feels that she could use support from a helpful adult to achieve a desired goal at school. If so, work with her to identify an adult she likes (for example, a neighbor, relative, or teacher) who might be interested in providing support.

Next, ask the student to think of a school goal she would like to achieve and to explain what she would need to do and not do to achieve the goal (for example, to be the possible academic self that she imagined earlier).

With the adult and the goal identified, help the student rehearse asking the adult for help with the goal and determine the best time and situation to make the request. When the student feels ready, have her implement the plan. If the adult is agreeable, ask him whether he or she thinks that goal selected is a good one (that is, challenging but doable and realistic—something the adult feels the student can accomplish). Explain that the adult needs to "buy in" to the goal if the adult is going to be an effective partner. If the adult has suggestions, therefore, ask the student to listen carefully and, where possible, to try to incorporate them.

With the plan set, ask the student to see whether the adult will meet on a regular basis to do as follows:

1. Help the student decide what she has to do, specifically, to accomplish the goal

2. Ensure that the student is actually doing what she needs to in order to accomplish the goal

3. Help gauge progress

4. Problem-solve if the student runs into trouble in accomplishing the goal

5. Celebrate with the student when she is successful

11.4 Using a "Looking Glass"

Explain to the youth that how he feels about himself as a student depends a lot on the messages he gets from important people in his life. Ask him to imagine that his caregivers and other kids are a "looking glass," or mirror.

Explain that he should pay attention to what they say and to notice their judgments about him as a student. Then, at the next session, ask him the following questions:

1. Did you get the same messages from both "mirrors"? For example, do caregivers and peers mirror back that you are a good student who tries hard, has good values, and is likely to be successful at school? Or do they mirror back that you are not so smart or not okay in some way—for example, either trying too little or too much with your schoolwork?

2. When you make a mistake or fail at school, what messages do you get from caregivers and other kids?

3. Do the messages suggest that caregivers and other kids see you as capable and expect you to do well?

Ask the student to consider and describe, in as much detail as possible, the messages he received from caregivers and other kids about his schoolwork this past week. The messages could be either direct (what someone actually said) or indirect (through facial expressions or jokes). Explain that jokes about a person often do not feel funny.

Ask the student whether the messages he received this past week:

1. Seemed clear, correct, and consistent

2. Made him feel good or bad

3. Affected his attitudes and actions in regard to schoolwork (for example, made him lose confidence, feel helpless, or want to give up)

4. Made him want to change how others look at his school behavior

If the student wants to try to change how others view him, brainstorm some ways it might be possible to do so and ask whether he is willing to give these ideas a try.

11.5   Assessing Peer Standards

Explain to the student that friends are likely to have a big effect on her beliefs about how important schoolwork is, how much effort she should make, and what she considers a good grade. Also point out that we tend to match the behavior of the people we spend the most time with. Therefore, how she acts in regard to schoolwork is likely to be influenced by the people she hangs out with.

Explain that in order to clarify how friendships might be affecting her school behavior and attitudes, you want her to choose up to three friends at school that she considers herself closest to and spends the most time with. Tell the student that you are going to give her the **Assessing Peer Standards** handout (Figure 23) about how those friends might be influencing her school behavior using her experiences over the past month.

FIGURE 23 Assessing Peer Standards

Choose up to three friends at school that you consider yourself close to and spend the most time with. Read the seven behaviors, and then place a check mark in the box if your friends did these things.

	Friend 1	Friend 2	Friend 3

This past month, my friend(s) . . .

	Friend 1	Friend 2	Friend 3
1. Got good grades	❑	❑	❑
2. Participated in class	❑	❑	❑
3. Did their homework	❑	❑	❑
4. Tried hard at school	❑	❑	❑
5. Paid attention	❑	❑	❑
6. Studied for tests	❑	❑	❑
7. Followed school rules	❑	❑	❑

Think about your actions during the past month and check the box next to anything that you did.

This past month, I . . .

1. Got good grades	❑
2. Participated in class	❑
3. Did my homework	❑
4. Tried hard at school	❑
5. Paid attention	❑
6. Studied for tests	❑
7. Followed school rules	❑

Based on the student's responses to the questions, ask:

1. What do your answers tell you?
2. How similar do you think you are to your friends in regard to your actions and attitudes about schoolwork?
3. How similar are your feelings about grades to those of your friends?
4. How much do you think your friends' actions and attitudes have affected your actions and attitudes?
5. Do you feel that your friends let you know whether they approve or disapprove of the way you act or feel about school? How can you tell?
6. Do you believe that how your friends view your grades has either a positive or negative effect on you (for example, makes you want to try harder or try less, affects how much you enjoy school)? How can you tell?

11.6   Getting Support from Friends

Tell the student that because friends can have an important effect on his ability to act the way he wants to act in relation to school, ask him to identify two or three friends who might be willing to form a buddy system with him to help each other keep to the standards they have set and accomplish school goals.

Discuss with the student how he might bring up the idea of a buddy system, and when. If the student has success in eliciting interest from some friends, suggest that they do the following:

1. Select a name for the group.
2. Pick individual goals to work toward (for example, improve grade in math by five points, get the science teacher to see that I am trying).
3. Discuss and write down in specific detail what each member needs to do, and not do, to achieve his goals (for example, study one-half hour each night and not play computer games during the school week until the goal is accomplished, hand in all homework on time).
4. Come up with a system for checking each other's efforts to stay on track.
5. Establish a regular meeting time to discuss progress.

Tell the student that you are available as a "consultant" to the group and can make suggestions to help them be as supportive and encouraging of each other as possible, if the members would like.

11.7   Using Schedules and To-Do Lists

Explain to the student that it is easier to keep to a plan to do schoolwork if she does these things:

1. Creates a record of what she has to do, either in an electronic organizer or on a piece of paper

2. Is specific when describing what needs to be done

3. Updates what needs to be done—and does so on a regular schedule (either in the evening or morning, or both)

4. Prioritizes and schedules the work by importance, urgency, or times when the particular type of task best fits her energy and alertness levels

5. Breaks tasks down into manageable parts

6. Writes down the due date, especially for long-term assignments

7. Monitors her time estimates relative to due dates and checks to make sure she is being realistic and making any needed adjustments in the pace of the work

Explain to the student that one way of telling whether a to-do list is working is if she does not feel panicked as a school assignment becomes due. Work with the student to develop a format for a daily to-do list, looking first at the school's to-do list if one is available. If the school has one, decide whether it needs to be modified to better match the student's specific needs.

Ask the student, for the upcoming week, to look at her to-do list at regular times to determine whether she has correctly estimated the time needed for tasks to be completed and has been able to stay on schedule—and whether doing so helps her feel like a good time and task manager. Also ask her to keep track of anything that might have interfered with adhering to her to-do list, such as lacking willpower, procrastinating, or dealing with unpredictable events.

Finally, ask the student to consider whether external reminders, such as an alarm on a watch or cell phone, might help her keep track of what she has to do. In a follow-up discussion, problem-solve as needed based on the results of the student's efforts and try to improve her use of the to-do list.

11.8   Assessing the Use of Routines

Explain to the student that he is more likely to enact strategies and maintain higher academic standards if he establishes routines and then follows these routines relatively automatically. To see how much the student now uses and keeps to routines, explain that you are going to ask him a series of questions from the **Assessing the Use of Routines** handout (Figure 24) and, based on his actions this past month. He should answer whether the statement is generally true or generally false.

Use the student's responses to discuss how the student:

1. Initially keeps track of what has to be done

2. Reviews his to-do list (if he uses one) before starting to work

3. Selects a time to start working

FIGURE 24   Assessing the Use of Routines

*Read each of the statements below. Circle **T** if it is true and **F** if it is false.*

1. I check to see what I have to do before I start to do it.   T   F

2. I do my homework at about the same time each day.   T   F

3. I do my homework in the same place each day.   T   F

4. I do my homework in the same order each day.   T   F

5. I make sure it is quiet as I do my homework.   T   F

6. I organize my materials before I start.   T   F

7. I check off each thing I complete when I complete it.   T   F

8. I put each completed assignment in my book bag when I complete it.   T   F

From *Self-Regulated Learning: Practical Strategies for Struggling Teens,* by Norman Brier, © 2010, Champaign, IL: Research Press (www.researchpress.com, 800-519-2707)

4. Gets the work done (does he work continuously, or does he work in starts and stops until the work is completed?)

5. Decides where to work (have him describe the setup of the homework space and the surrounding environment)

6. Decides the order of work to be done (for example, randomly, by due date, the same order by subject every night)

7. Checks off or keeps track of what he has finished

8. Decides what he does with completed work to get it ready to be handed in

Highlight, again, both the importance of employing set routines, particularly routines that make it more likely that boring or repetitive school tasks will be completed, and the value of working in an organized, distraction-free space.

Use the student's responses to discuss ways he might improve keeping track of assignments, scheduling work time, and selecting and setting up a place to work. As part of the discussion, ask the student how he estimates the time needed to complete an assignment and how he prioritizes school tasks so that assignments can be carried out in a predictable order (for example, using categories such as earliest to latest deadlines or easiest to hardest school subject to create an order for doing the work). Also address how the student allocates his time and schedules long-term assignments.

Together with the student, design an ideal routine and ask whether he is willing to try it for one week. Ask him to keep track of times when he was not able to keep to the routine, so that when you discuss how things went, you and he can make improvements. When you meet next time, review the results and modify the plan as needed.

11.9　Preventing Tasks from Becoming Boring

Explain that while routines can be very helpful in getting things done, doing the same thing in the same way, over and over again, can become boring—and, when activities become boring, it is hard to stay interested and motivated. It is important, therefore, to find ways to make school tasks more interesting so that the student can stay motivated and achieve her goals.

Tell the student that you have a list of things that other student have done to keep schoolwork interesting. Explain that you are going to review these ideas with her to see whether she is willing to try some of them.

Read and discuss the ideas on the **Ways to Sustain Interest** handout (Figure 25) to sustain interest and avoid boredom. Ask the student to pick the ideas that she feels might work best for her and try one or two of them the next time she gets bored or loses interest in a task. Tell the student that you will ask her next time whether she tried any of the ideas and, if so, how well they worked.

FIGURE 25   Ways to Sustain Interest

When you find yourself becoming bored by schoolwork, try some of these ideas.

1. Develop ways to measure whether you are improving (for example, checking assignments off as you complete them and putting them in a specified folder in your book bag) and assess your progress as you are doing your work.

2. Intentionally increase the difficulty of a task so that it is more challenging but still doable.

3. Give yourself a reward for completing a task (for example, ice cream or time doing something you want to do when finished).

4. Add something stimulating to the situation so that you feel more alert (for example, play some music quietly in the background).

5. Before starting a task, think about how the task relates to your present or future life so that the task feels more relevant and useful.

6. Try to relate the task to something you enjoy or find interesting.

7. See whether you can make a game out of the task.

8. Take short breaks for a preplanned period of time.

9. In a planned way, periodically change the time or place you do a task.

10. Remind yourself why it is a good idea to do the work.

Review and Key Ideas Challenge

OVERVIEW

This chapter provides an opportunity for the student to consolidate learning by identifying the factors identified in this book as being associated with academic self-regulation. The vehicle for identification is an extended story about John. While it is unlikely that any single student would employ all of these self-regulation techniques in such a short time span, John's story offers a challenging means of review as well as another opportunity to discuss what methods work for individual students. (Appendix B provides answer keys to the challenge.)

Academic Self-Regulation Defined

The term *academic self-regulation* refers to a student's ability to exert and maintain self-control while attempting to achieve academic goals (Zimmerman & Schunk, 2008). Students who demonstrate higher levels of academic self-regulation can set academic objectives and standards; create strategies to attain the objectives and standards that they have set; monitor their actions and progress to ensure that they stay on track; note discrepancies between their behavior and intentions, and, based on this feedback, adjust their actions when necessary to better match their intentions (Carver & Scheier, 1982; Hoeksma, Oosterlaan, & Schipper, 2004).

The Critical Role of Choice

For students to demonstrate academic self-regulation, they must have the opportunity to select their academic goals, establish standards of acceptable performance, determine the amount of effort that they are willing to expend, and choose strategies to accomplish their goals and maintain their standards. Through the process of making choices, students learn to appreciate the relationships among their intentions, decisions, and actions, and the consequences that ensue. As a result, they are more likely to develop a sense of accountability for their academic behavior and to take responsibility for the outcomes that follow (Deci & Ryan, 1985; Skinner & Edge, 2002). When faced with a choice, students' values, or idea of what is an important and desirable end state and way of acting, play an important role (Rokeach, 1973), as does their capacity to maintain willpower. Students differ both in their readiness to make choices and their ability to exert willpower, follow through, and stay committed to their choices, particularly when frustrated (Prochaska, 1979).

The actions of parents and teachers can facilitate or undermine a student's autonomy or responsibility for making choices. Students display higher levels of academic self-regulation and experience an increased sense of ownership in regard to their schoolwork when caregivers collaborate—that is, allow them to state their perspective and feelings and give them a significant degree of influence in selecting academic goals and strategies (Deci & Ryan, 1985).

Goals, Expectations, Value, and Interest

There are important differences between intentions and goals. Although they both involve a desire to achieve a purpose, goals include details about how something is to be attained. These specifics include actions that need to occur to indicate that the purpose has been achieved, as well as time frames and strategies for achieving it. Therefore, goals, unlike intentions, provide a structure to help organize behavior, encourage a focus on goal-relevant information, enhance accountability, and provide a means to track progress and obtain feedback, thereby triggering the use of self-correcting behavior (Deci, Ryan, & Williams, 1996; Zimmerman, 2008).

Goals can be differentiated by their intent. The intent of a goal can be to achieve a positive outcome or avoid a negative one, impress others, achieve a personally meaningful end, or accomplish something in the short- or long-term (Zimmerman, 2008). Regardless of the particular intent of a goal, students are more likely to work to achieve their goals if they perceive their goals as useful, relevant, or important (Eccles, Wigfield, & Schiefele, 2002). They are also more likely to achieve their goals if they are able to focus on the future as well as the present. By focusing on the future (that is, having a future time perspective), students can visualize the benefits that might result if they attain their goals and thus are better able to justify the effort needed in the present to achieve those benefits in the future (Simons et al., 2004).

A student's expectations about the likelihood of achieving an academic goal strongly affect her level of academic self-regulation. These expectations are based, in large part, on the student's perceptions of her past academic achievements, her level of self-confidence, her beliefs about the difficulty of the current academic task, and the attitudes and expectations conveyed to her by important adults, particularly parents and teachers (Wigfield & Eccles, 1992). The student's expectations, in turn, strongly influence the amount of effort and persistence she will exert. Students who expect to succeed tend to exert high levels of effort, intensify their effort when encountering an obstacle, and persist until successful. On the other hand, students who expect to fail tend to exert low levels of effort, are easily discouraged, and cease trying in the face of frustration (Bandura & Cervone, 1983).

The degree to which students view an academic task as valuable also influences their level of academic self-regulation (Wigfield & Eccles, 1992). Thus, students tend to exert more effort and be more disciplined when academic tasks are perceived as valuable (Wigfield, 1994a, 1994b) and thought to lead to desirable incentives (Rokeach, 1973). Interest is a key determinant of the degree of value a student will attach to an academic task (Eccles & Parsons, 1983). When interested, students tend to be more engaged and attentive and, as a result, are more likely to achieve their academic goals (Hidi & Ainley, 2008).

Planning

To be academically self-regulated, students need to plan (Zimmerman, 2008). They need to carefully select strategies, then detail and sequence these strategies on a time line. Students who plan are more likely to maintain self-control when pursuing academic goals and are better able to track when, where, and how academic tasks need to be performed. As a result, they are more likely to be successful in achieving their academic goals (Pressley & Woloshyn, 1995). One especially important part of planning involves knowing when to seek help, thinking about whom to ask for help, and rehearsing what to say while asking (Newman, 2008).

Academic Self-Concept and Self-Efficacy

Students who have a positive academic self-concept and feel efficacious are more likely to carry out their academic plans and persist until they are successful. Students with positive beliefs about their academic competence and ability to be successful tend to exhibit higher levels of energy, effort, and persistence (Eccles & Parsons, 1983). Beliefs about academic competence are strongly influenced by a student's perceptions of her past and present academic successes and failures and by the feedback she receives from the important people in her life.

The quality of a student's academic self-concept depends, in part, on her explanations and beliefs about why she succeeded or failed. A student is likely to have a poor academic self-concept, and not feel self-efficacious, if she attributes past failures to internal and stable causes ("I am so stupid!"). On the other hand, a student is likely to have a positive academic self-concept, and feel self-efficacious, if she attributes past academic outcomes to a controllable cause, such as effort. Attributing success to a controllable cause allows the student to believe that continued success is always possible if she engages in the necessary behavior (Weiner, 1986).

Attributions about intelligence have an especially powerful effect on a student's academic self-concept and sense of self-efficacy. Students who believe that they have a fixed amount of intelligence, and who attribute poor school performance to a lack of intelligence, tend to lose motivation. They often feel that there is little that they can do to improve the situation, are more likely to be self-critical, and either give up easily or avoid attempting difficult school tasks. In addition, when students see themselves as "dumb," they often develop feelings of learned helplessness—they believe that nothing they do will result in success (Seligman, 1975). On the other hand, students who believe that intelligence is malleable tend to feel that, with effort, they can make incremental, positive improvements. As a result, they tend to be more motivated to achieve academic goals, take on challenging learning tasks, show initiative, and exert effort and persistence while doing so (Ommundsen, Haugen, & Lund, 2005).

A student's image of how she wants to be, or feels she ought to be, is also likely to affect academic self-regulation. When doing schoolwork, students tend to act consistently with the self-attributions that they consider important, and they avoid acting in ways that are inconsistent with these self-attributions. Thus, the image of how the student wants to be, or believes she ought to be, tends to function as a self-guide—a reference standard that helps the student define what constitutes desirable and acceptable academic goals and standards (Higgins, 1991). In addition, self-attributions help the student imagine and define a wished-for "possible self" that she could attain with effort and persistence (Markus & Nurius, 1986). Once a student develops a possible self and internal guidelines to attain it, she can evaluate her actions according to those guidelines and, when necessary, adjust her actions, aspirations, or self-guide accordingly (Pham & Taylor, 1999). When a student considers both short-term and long-term goals when visualizing her aspirations, she creates a path that connects the present to the future, thereby increasing the likelihood that future academic goals will be perceived as tangible and attainable (Oyserman et al., 2004).

Self-Monitoring and Attention Management

To achieve valued academic goals, proficiency in self-monitoring is required. While performing academic tasks, students need to be aware of, and systematically track, the degree to which their behavior is goal relevant and matches their standards. If discrepancies are observed, students must be able to enact self-corrections and then observe whether these self-corrective actions are successful in moving them along the path toward their academic goals (Carver & Scheier, 1982).

The ability to allocate and manage attention is central to self-monitoring. Students need to be able to selectively attend to goal-relevant information, stay vigilant, and sustain their focus as they work to achieve their academic goals (Reid, 1996). Pre-planning facilitates this process. Students are more likely to consider their academic goals, standards, and strategies when they develop detailed mental representations of their intended actions, including the cues that they will use as reminders, and select carefully the time and place that they will enact academic tasks. Students who pre-plan are more likely to focus on the specific aspects of situations that relate to attaining their academic goals, retrieve the pertinent information, sustain their attention, and resist distractions (Gollwitzer, 1999). Students are more likely to be proficient at self-monitoring when they use a recording method to track their progress (Reid, 1996), particularly when they include carefully defined objective criteria to indicate success, use preset times to record their progress, and follow specific guidelines about what they will record (Shapiro & Cole, 1999).

Skill in attention management is determined, in part, by the student's language competence, particularly in using private speech (Meichenbaum, 1977). An ability to employ such phrases as "What's my goal in this situation?" "I need to concentrate and stay on task" and "Am I acting in the way I should?" helps students identify relevant internal and external cues, as well as the salience of task attributes and academic goals. In addition, when skilled in using private speech, students can create a guide that helps them direct their attention as they engage in an academic task, facilitate their retrieval of pertinent information, resist focusing on extraneous information, and self-monitor (Vygotsky, 1962).

Mood and Anxiety

The ability to exert and maintain self-control while attempting to achieve academic goals is strongly affected by mood and level of anxiety (Gendolla & Brinkman, 2005). Mood influences action, the ability to manage attention and process information, and the capacity to mobilize and direct effort. In addition, the mood a student is experiencing at a given time influences how rewarding and interesting she will judge a task to be, as well as her level of self-confidence and perceptions about the difficulty of the task (Blair, 2002). Further, when in a negative mood, students can become overaroused and attend to the source of their distress rather than to goal-relevant information (Derryberry & Reed, 2002). In addition, they are likely to feel less self-efficacious and more likely to believe that they have little influence over academic outcomes (Bandura, 1997).

Anxiety can also interfere with academic self-regulation by diminishing a student's ability to stay focused on academic goals. When excessively worried, nervous, fearful, or self-conscious, students tend to divide their attention between task-relevant and anxiety-linked thoughts, focus on aspects of academic situations that relate to the possibility of failure, and, as a result, avoid academic tasks or fail to persist at them (Lewis, 1992).

Anxiety is commonly expressed by procrastination—anxious students tend to put off academic tasks that they need to complete. Perfectionism, at times, also creates anxiety and interferes with the ability to be academically self-regulated. Perfectionistic students set unrealistically high academic standards, worry excessively about making mistakes, ruminate about possible errors, and postpone or avoid doing work out of fear that they will fail to meet their too-high standards (Shafran & Mansell, 2001).

The Social and Physical Context

Academic self-regulation is enhanced when caregivers encourage autonomy, display interest, provide support, convey acceptance, and maintain high expectations for academic success (Eisenberg et al., 2001). Academic self-regulation is also enhanced when caregivers are able to modulate their own emotional reactions to their students' academic behavior and when they allow the students to perform schoolwork as autonomously as possible (Deci, Ryan, & Williams, 1996).

The physical and social contexts also play an important role in academic self-regulation. Academic self-regulation is relatively high when the home environment is organized, distraction free, and predictable and includes information, feedback, and strategies to achieve desired academic outcomes (Logan, 1988). Likewise, peers can exert influence on a student's academic self-regulation. Students tend to match, or model, the academic aspirations of their peers. Students use their perceptions of their peers' values to compare and define their own standards of acceptable academic behavior. Students are also likely to demonstrate higher levels of academic self-regulation when their peers possess values that support school success and demonstrate behavior that makes academic success more likely (Oyserman & Terry, 2006).

INTERVENTIONS

12.1   Key Ideas Associated with Self-Regulation

Explain to the student that, as a review of the main ideas that have been discussed, you are going to present a challenge: You are going to read a story about someone named John who tries to improve his self-regulation while doing schoolwork. Explain that key ideas about self-regulation and academic success have been written into this story.

Read **John's Story** (Figure 26) aloud, then provide the student a copy of the story and the **Key Ideas Associated with Academic Self-Regulation** handout (Figure 27). In the text of the story, short passages are underlined. Each underlined passage is preceded by a letter or letters. Ask the student to read the story again, to himself this time, and pay attention to the underlined text. As he works, he should try to find the key idea on the list that best matches the underlined text. Once he matches an underlined passage with the corresponding key idea, he should write the letter or letters preceding the underlined words in the space before its corresponding idea on the list of key ideas.

Explain to the student that if he gets stuck, you will help. Also, if any of the key ideas seem confusing to him, tell the student to let you know and you will explain the idea. If the student has trouble reading, read the underlined words with him and work together to find the matching key ideas.

When the student has done the best he can, use the answer key in Appendix B to review his answers with him. Explain any omitted or incorrect answers by reviewing and discussing the relevant parts of the story.

12.2   Postintervention Assessment

Remind the student about the activity presented in the introduction to this book in which she pretended that she was a scientist collecting data about how well she does in setting goals, selecting strategies, and monitoring her school work (intervention 1.1). Give the student a blank copy of the **Academic Self-Regulation Checklist** from Appendix A or the CD, review its contents, and ask her to complete the checklist again, this time based on her actions and activities over the past month. Explain that you and she will now have "data" to determine what has changed since she completed the checklist the first time and what areas might need additional work.

After the student completes the checklist, review and discuss how her answers on the initial checklist compare with her current answers. Give honest feedback, starting with the positive changes she has made in regard to academic self-regulation, followed by what she still might need to work on. Discuss with the student her "stage of change"—how ready and willing she seems to be to work on these tasks—and plan follow-up activities accordingly.

FIGURE 26   John's Story

1   Told that he had to sit for one hour at his desk in detention, John had a lot of time to think. He thought about how he would get the usual lecture from his father about the importance of school and how he was having trouble finding a new job because he does not have a college degree. John was also wondering about what the assistant principal wanted to tell him. She said that she needed to see him after detention. And, instead of being friendly like she usually was, she seemed upset with him. Maybe, he thought, it is because this was his third detention this month.

2   Even before his father was laid off and everyone was nervous and sad at home, (**A**) John couldn't get himself to work hard at school; the schoolwork just seemed so unimportant this year. He would try to listen to his social studies teacher, Mr. Samuels, for example, talk about Abraham Lincoln, (**B**) but John could not see how a famous speech from a long time ago was relevant to the things that were going on right now. The feeling of boredom kept getting stronger—and he had started to come to class late and forget to do a lot of his homework assignments.

3   Deep in thought, John did not hear when the assistant principal, Ms. Campbell, entered the detention room. She said, "Follow me to my office, John" and did not speak again until she sat down and asked him to take the chair across from her.

4   "Last year," she began, "you were a good student. If you remember, you said to me that (**C**) school was valuable to you, and you said you wanted to work hard so you could get on the high honor roll. You made me a bet that by the end of the year, your name would be on the list. At the end of the year, you won the bet, and I was proud of you. If you remember, I bought you the book on caring for pets, a special interest of yours, as a reward (**D**) because I was so impressed when I heard from your teachers that even when you were frustrated, you showed good self-control while you worked and kept at things until you were successful.

5   "This year, all your teachers tell me that you (**E**) act as if you feel that schoolwork is not useful to you at all. (**F**) If you do hand in an assignment, you either hand it in late, or incorrect, as if you are not really paying attention to the instructions. (**G**) Your teachers tell me that when they ask you about homework, you say to them that you will hand in what is due but then keep putting off doing the work—and never do it. Instead, you just keep making excuses as to why you can't. I know that things are tough for you at home since your dad has been laid off, but I am not going to let a bright student like you—someone who can accomplish so much—act like a loser. I talked to your parents and the principal. (**H**) We all agreed that by the end of the school year, three months from now, you have to achieve several goals: You need to get passing grades in every class, hand in all your assignments on time, and follow the instructions for each assignment completely and correctly. If you do not achieve all three goals, you will not be promoted.

From *Self-Regulated Learning: Practical Strategies for Struggling Teens,* by Norman Brier, © 2010, Champaign, IL: Research Press (www.researchpress.com, 800-519-2707)

Figure 26 (p. 2 of 4)

6   "There is one more thing. The owner of the Pet Emporium called me and said he wants an assistant to help feed and take care of the pets after school, three days a week, for two hours each day. I spoke about this idea with your parents, and they said it was okay with them if you want to take the job. They also know that, as "pay," the store owner would give your family a $30 gift certificate each week that can be used to buy food at the supermarket. If you decide to take the job, you would have to work very hard and be very responsible. Think over what I said, and tomorrow I want you to tell me your thoughts and your decision about the job offer."

7   As John walked out of Ms. Campbell's office and started home, he felt scared about what his parents would say when he got home but also grown-up that he would be helping them by working at the pet store. (**I**) <u>He thought about how Ms. Campbell said he is bright but that he had been acting like a loser. He thought she was right. He had been making very bad choices lately. He remembered how important it was last year to do his schoolwork well and get on the honor roll. He remembered how he had hoped his parents would be pleased if he got very good grades and pictured how happy they actually were when he got them.</u> (**J**) <u>John had confidence that if he put forth a lot of effort and stayed focused on his goals, he would be successful.</u>

8   John tried to imagine what the next few weeks would be like. (**K**) <u>He pictured straightening out his stuff, keeping his desk neat and organized so he could find what he needed, and starting his work the same time each day.</u> If he was not going to mess up and forget something, he thought, he probably also (**L**) <u>needed to create routines and do the work in the same order each day</u> and be extra careful about paying attention to what the assignment actually said. (**M**) <u>He also tried to imagine that it was the end of June. He pictured Ms. Campbell congratulating him and saying, "I knew you could accomplish so much if you tried," and his parents hugging him and telling him that they were proud of him for helping his family out and showing how bright he was. It was really important to John to make this picture come true.</u>

9   When he got home, John's parents were waiting for him. Instead of being angry, they asked him to tell them what he heard Ms. Campbell say in order to be sure that everyone had the same understanding. John started talking, and to his surprise, began to cry. Tearfully, he explained that school seemed to be a waste of time and that each night, instead of doing his homework, he would play on the computer. His parents said, "We are a family, and we will work together to get things back to the way they should be. (**N**) <u>If you want to take this job, you can, but only if you are sure that you can keep up with your schoolwork. We are not going to tell you what to do about the job. After supper, we want to hear your thoughts and help you make a good decision.</u>" They also mentioned that Aunt Jane, his mom's sister who taught at another school, offered to help John if he wants her to.

10 After supper, John told his parents that it was very important to him to take the job at the Pet Emporium, and he felt that he could do the job and also do well at school. John went on to say that to be sure that he did his best, he would accept Aunt Jane's help.

Figure 26 (p. 3 of 4)

His parents said okay. The next day, at school, John said to Ms. Campbell that he would take the pet store job. He also told her that he would like to again bet her that not only would he pass all his classes, he would be on the very high honor roll by the end of June. Ms. Campbell said that she would be glad to make the bet again and that she would call the owner of the pet store to tell him that John would start work on Monday.

11   That weekend, he met with his Aunt Jane. She helped him make a schedule so that he could keep track of what he had to do. She explained that (**O**) John might keep track of the assignments that he has to complete and the specific ways that he hopes to act in order to feel as proud of himself as possible and keep comparing these ideal ways of acting with how he actually acts. John thought about what Aunt Jane said and (**P**) imagined himself as someone who creates specific, very detailed strategies to get his work done and carefully writes down assignments, checks to be sure that the assignments have been done correctly, and remembers to pay attention in class. Aunt Jane asked him to (**Q**) write the ways he hopes to act on a piece of paper. She explained that people usually keep to a plan better if they use a recording system and check on how they are doing regularly—that is, self-monitor their behavior at specific times each day.

12   On Monday, John was able to act the way he had hoped to in school but had trouble concentrating. He couldn't stop thinking about starting his new job right after school. Finally, the school day ended and he went to the pet store. The owner, who introduced himself as Dan, told John that he had a very important job. (**R**) He told John it was important that he focus on what he needed to accomplish at the pet store to be a good worker, and explained that John had only two jobs: keeping the cages very clean and feeding the pets—making sure each pet got the right food. As his Aunt Jane did, Dan suggested that John make a list of the things that he had to do, and the order that he would do them in, so that he would not make a mistake. As he started cleaning the cages, John (**S**) felt very responsible for the living things that he would be taking care of. Because being a kind person was so important to John, he wanted to think of ways that he could be very good at caring for the pets. He decided to write on a piece of paper: "Be an extra-careful worker" and look at the saying each hour on the hour and then make sure he had done the things that he was supposed to do. (**T**) He also planned to do each of his jobs in the same sequence and at the same time each day.

13   At school each day, (**U**) John monitored his progress to see whether he was achieving the goals that the teachers had set, and he regularly compared how he was acting with the way he wanted to act. He felt happy with how he was doing up until Friday. Thursday evening, when his parents thought that he was asleep, he had heard them talking about how worried they were about being able to pay the bills that month. Earlier in the week, before he had overheard his parents' conversation about bills, (**V**) John had been able to keep his attention focused while doing schoolwork by saying such things to himself as "I need to act like an honor

Figure 26 (p. 4 of 4)

student," "Look carefully at the directions," and "Did I skip anything?" (**W**) <u>He also had been able to notice cues in the classroom to remind himself of what he needed to do, and he had especially been good at noting the assignments that the teacher wrote on the top right side of the board.</u>

14   On Friday in math class, though, he kept thinking about his parents' words and felt upset. (**X**) <u>John realized pretty quickly that he was not paying attention as he had intended to. He felt happy that he was able to see right away the difference between how he wanted to act and how he was actually acting,</u> and (**Y**) <u>he remembered a technique that a teacher had described to help calm down. She had said that he should focus on his breathing and clear his mind. John tried to do just what the teacher had demonstrated—and it worked. He actually felt calmer and could focus.</u> (**Z**) <u>John was able to quickly solve the math problems that the teacher had written on the board. He felt proud of himself. He thought, "I am a very good math student." He also felt proud that he had realized so quickly that he was distracted, and he felt confident that if he needed to calm down in the future, he could do so by using that breathing technique.</u>

15   Work that Friday also did not go well. John loved almost everything about the job except one part—poop. He hated to clean up the poop in the cages and would keep putting it off. When Dan noticed that it was getting late and John had not yet cleaned the cages, he reminded John that he had to keep to the order of the tasks on the list. (**AA**) <u>John thought he needed Dan's advice to help him do what he was supposed to do. He carefully thought about what he wanted to ask Dan and the best time to ask for his help. When he saw that Dan was not busy, he approached him and asked whether Dan could suggest a way that John would not put off the unpleasant task that they had discussed.</u> Dan suggested that he do the unpleasant task first and get it over with. From then on, that is what John did.

16   As the days passed, John found that (**BB**) <u>he was again liking school, especially science, and saw that because he was interested in what the teacher was talking about, it was now easy to pay attention.</u> It also seemed easier and easier for John to remember to do the things that he had to do at school, do them correctly, and (**CC**) <u>notice and feel proud of himself when he did something right.</u> Best of all, his dad had been called back to work, and his parents no longer seemed worried about paying the bills.

17   In the last week in June, when the teachers handed in the grades, Ms. Campbell called John into her office. In a teasing way, she asked John to guess whether he thought he won their bet. John said he was not sure but hoped he had. She said, in fact, he had won the bet and that she was very proud of him. She asked John what he thought he had learned from this year. John paused before answering and said, (**DD**) <u>"It is up to me if I am good at school. If I try hard and put forth a lot of effort, I can be successful.</u> (**EE**) <u>I also learned that I can always improve my abilities if I plan carefully, pick good strategies, and work hard.</u> (**FF**) <u>And, I see that I am responsible for how things go—I can either choose to do my best or not. It is up to me."</u>

FIGURE 27   Key Ideas Associated with Academic Self-Regulation

Academic self-regulation is likely to be improved when . . .

_____ 1. The student's home environment is organized and predictable.

_____ 2. The student uses a recording system as part of self-monitoring—and the system includes specific behaviors to be tracked and states a schedule for when self-monitoring will occur.

_____ 3. The student thinks about the personal characteristics that he or she values the most when selecting goals and standards

_____ 4. The student plans which tasks to do, in what order, and when.

_____ 5. The student sees the schoolwork as useful.

_____ 6. The student makes note of any differences between his or her intentions and actual behavior.

_____ 7. The student exerts willpower and self-control while performing schoolwork.

_____ 8. The student does not put off doing tasks.

_____ 9. The student selects cues as reminders to carry out his or her strategies.

_____ 10. The student views ability as something that can be improved with effort and the right strategy.

_____ 11. The student thinks that academic tasks are interesting.

_____ 12. The student's goals include a clear definition of success and the time when success will be achieved.

_____ 13. The student establishes and follows a routine.

_____ 14. The student focuses on what he or she does right when doing schoolwork.

_____ 15. The student understands the need to stay focused on information relevant to achieving his or her goals.

_____ 16. The student considers schoolwork to be important—and is thereby more motivated to apply effort.

_____ 17. The student sees academic tasks as valuable and leading to future rewards or benefits.

_____ 18. The student's parents, teachers, and other important adults are not over-controlling and allow collaboration.

_____ 19. The student creates specific, detailed strategies to achieve goals.

_____ 20. The student can calm himself or herself when distressed while doing school-work and can stay focused on what he or she needs to learn.

_____ 21. The student regularly monitors his or her actual behavior at school and compare it with what he or she wants to do (or feels he or she ought to do).

From *Self-Regulated Learning: Practical Strategies for Struggling Teens,* by Norman Brier, © 2010, Champaign, IL: Research Press (www.researchpress.com, 800-519-2707)

Figure 27 (p. 2 of 2)

_____ 22. The student is confident in his or her abilities and has a positive image about himself or herself as a student.

_____ 23. The student expects to be successful.

_____ 24. The student thinks about what is valuable or important in doing a good job on schoolwork.

_____ 25. The student can think about the end point of a task—that is, he or she can answer the question "What do I want to accomplish?"

_____ 26. The student uses private speech to help manage and control his or her attention while doing school tasks.

_____ 27. The student thinks about a possible "academic self" and compares his or her actions to those of the possible academic self.

_____ 28. The student thinks before asking for help and considers whom to ask, when to ask, and what to ask.

_____ 29. The student regularly visualizes future academic successes and the benefits that will occur as a result.

_____ 30. The student is allowed to make choices in regard to schoolwork—and therefore feels more accountable.

_____ 31. The student is engaged in schoolwork and sees it as relevant to his or her concerns.

_____ 32. The student believes that effort is critical to academic success and thinks that a positive outcome is within his or her control.

Academic Self-Regulation Checklist

To score the Academic Self-Regulation Checklist, tally each column and then add to obtain a total score. (Items with an asterisk are reverse-scored.) When used to assess the effectiveness of the intervention, a change in scores between two administrations can indicate the direction of change (whether positive or negative) and provide a very rough estimate of the degree of change.

The checklist can also provide valuable diagnostic information. By carefully examining the student's responses to individual items and how responses cluster, you can identify the student's strengths and weaknesses and target remedial plans accordingly—for example, emphasizing motivation or attention management.

Scores on the checklist can range from 62 to 186. Low scores, based on the reported infrequency of academic self-regulation skills, suggest relatively poor academic self-regulation skills, and high scores suggest relatively adequate academic self-regulation skills. Pending standardization studies of the checklist to allow norm-referenced interpretations of scores, scores should be used primarily to provide qualitative information and a gross estimate of the student's level of academic self-regulation.

Academic Self-Regulation Checklist

Read each statement and then check the box that best describes how often the statement applies to you.

	Almost never	Sometimes	Almost always
1. I think about why I should do my schoolwork before I start doing it.	❏	❏	❏
2. I give thought to how well I am doing at school.	❏	❏	❏
3. I think that how well I do at school is mostly up to me.	❏	❏	❏
4. If I get stuck doing my schoolwork, I feel I can eventually figure out what to do.	❏	❏	❏
5. How much effort I put forth determines how well I do at school.	❏	❏	❏
6. I can figure out what I did that resulted in receiving a particular grade.	❏	❏	❏
7. When schoolwork is difficult, I work hard and keep at it until I finish.	❏	❏	❏
8. Being successful at school is important to me, and I will work hard to be successful.	❏	❏	❏
9. When I start my schoolwork, I expect to be able to do it well.	❏	❏	❏
10. If I pay attention, I can understand the work, even if it is difficult.	❏	❏	❏
11. I can guess correctly how well I am doing at school.	❏	❏	❏
12. I try to do well at school so I can feel proud of the progress that I make.	❏	❏	❏
13. I like difficult schoolwork because it gets me to try my best.	❏	❏	❏
14. When schoolwork is boring, I can figure out ways of keeping at it until I finish.	❏	❏	❏

From *Self-Regulated Learning: Practical Strategies for Struggling Teens,* by Norman Brier, © 2010, Champaign, IL: Research Press (www.researchpress.com, 800-519-2707)

	Almost never	Sometimes	Almost always
15. Doing well at school is important to me.	❑	❑	❑
16. What I learn in school will help me when I am an adult.	❑	❑	❑
17. What I learn in school will help me at home or with friends.	❑	❑	❑
18. I feel interested in things that I learn at school.	❑	❑	❑
19. Before I start my work, I take time to figure out what I have to do so I can do it correctly.	❑	❑	❑
20. I have a routine for homework and do my work at the same time and place each day.	❑	❑	❑
21. Before I start my homework, I make a plan about the order in which I will do it.	❑	❑	❑
22. Before I start my homework, I figure out how much time I will need to do each task.	❑	❑	❑
23. When I get back a test, I compare the test score with my mental image of how I want to be as a student.	❑	❑	❑
24. I use the mental image of how I would like to be as a student to decide how hard I want to work.	❑	❑	❑
25. I have a clear picture of what I need to do to be a really good student.	❑	❑	❑
26. I know someone who has done very well at school that I admire and would like to be like.	❑	❑	❑
27. I think about how well I would like to do before I start an important school project.	❑	❑	❑
28. I keep my good intentions about school in my mind and think about them.	❑	❑	❑
29. I think about ways I could do better at school.	❑	❑	❑
30. I keep track of how much of a long-term assignment I have completed as I do the assignment.	❑	❑	❑
31. I write down in a particular place what I have to remember to do for school.	❑	❑	❑

	Almost never	Sometimes	Almost always
32. I catch myself when my attention wanders and can refocus on my schoolwork.	❏	❏	❏
33. I can get myself to pay attention at school, even when the work is not interesting.	❏	❏	❏
34. I can say things to myself to help me keep doing what I am supposed to do.	❏	❏	❏
35. Before I leave school, I make sure I know what homework I have and what materials I will need.	❏	❏	❏
36. When I finish my schoolwork, I check to see that I did it all.	❏	❏	❏
37. When I finish my schoolwork, I check to see that I did it correctly.	❏	❏	❏
38. I keep track of the time as I do my work to make sure I will finish everything.	❏	❏	❏
39. I change how I am doing my work if I am getting distracted or not getting it done correctly.	❏	❏	❏
40. When I do well at school, I feel proud; when I do poorly, I feel ashamed or embarrassed.	❏	❏	❏
41. I ask for help if I see that I am having trouble finishing my work or am doing it incorrectly.	❏	❏	❏
42. My nervous feelings at school make it hard to concentrate on my schoolwork.*	❏	❏	❏
43. When I feel sad at school, my schoolwork does not seem important.*	❏	❏	❏
44. I feel tired at school and do not have the energy to do my work.*	❏	❏	❏
45. When I take a test, I worry a lot about how I will do.*	❏	❏	❏
46. I worry a lot that I will do badly at school.*	❏	❏	❏

	Almost never	Sometimes	Almost always
47. I have to get really high grades to feel satisfied that I am doing okay at school.*	❑	❑	❑
48. I put off my schoolwork till the last minute.*	❑	❑	❑
49. If I feel that I am not going to do my work well, I avoid doing it.	❑	❑	❑
50. I think a lot about how kids at school do not like me and then have trouble concentrating on my work.*	❑	❑	❑
51. I get very upset at school and have trouble calming down.*	❑	❑	❑
52. My parent(s) get really angry when we talk about school.*	❑	❑	❑
53. My parent(s) criticize me when I don't do well at school.*	❑	❑	❑
54. My parent(s) try to understand why I have gotten a particular grade before they tell me their thoughts.	❑	❑	❑
55. My parent(s) want to help me with my schoolwork, even if they think I have not done my best.	❑	❑	❑
56. My parent(s) let me do my work on my own and help me only when I ask for help.	❑	❑	❑
57. My parent(s) would fight for me if something happened at school that was not fair.	❑	❑	❑
58. My friends work hard at school.	❑	❑	❑
59. My friends do their homework and study for tests.	❑	❑	❑
60. My friends are proud of their good grades.	❑	❑	❑
61. I do my homework in a quiet place.	❑	❑	❑
62. I keep the place where I do my homework neat and organized.	❑	❑	❑
Totals	____ +	____ +	____ = ____

Answer Keys

1 Told that he had to sit for one hour at his desk in detention, John had a lot of time to think. He thought about how he would get the usual lecture from his father about the importance of school and how he was having trouble finding a new job because he does not have a college degree. John was also wondering about what the assistant principal wanted to tell him. She said that she needed to see him after detention. And, instead of being friendly like she usually was, she seemed upset with him. Maybe, he thought, it is because this was his third detention this month.

2 Even before his father was laid off and everyone was nervous and sad at home, (A) John couldn't get himself to work hard at school; the schoolwork just seemed so unimportant this year [16].He would try to listen to his social studies teacher, Mr. Samuels, for example, talk about Abraham Lincoln, (B) but John could not see how a famous speech from a long time ago was relevant to the things that were going on right now [31]. The feeling of boredom kept getting stronger—and he had started to come to class late and forget to do a lot of his homework assignments.

3 Deep in thought, John did not hear when the assistant principal, Ms. Campbell, entered the detention room. She said, "Follow me to my office, John" and did not speak again until she sat down and asked him to take the chair across from her.

4 "Last year," she began, "you were a good student. If you remember, you said to me that (C) school was valuable to you, and you said you wanted to work hard so you could get on the high honor roll. You made me a bet that by the end of the year, your name would be on the list [17]. At the end of the year, you won the bet, and I was proud of you. If you remember, I bought you the book on caring for pets, a special interest of yours, as a reward (D) because I was so impressed when I heard from your teachers that even when you were frustrated, you showed good self-control while you worked and kept at things until you were successful [7].

5 "This year, all your teachers tell me that you (E) act as if you feel that schoolwork is not useful to you at all [5]. (F) If you do hand in an assignment, you either hand it in late, or incorrect, as if you are not really paying attention to the instructions [15]. (G) Your teachers tell me that when they ask you about homework, you say to them that you will hand in what is due but then keep putting off doing the work—and never do it. Instead, you just keep making excuses as to why you can't [8]. I know that things are tough for you at home since your dad has been laid off, but I am not going to let a bright student like you—someone who can accomplish so much—act like a loser. I talked to your parents and the principal. (H) We all agreed that by the end of the school year, three months from now, you have to achieve several goals: You need to get passing grades in every class, hand in all your assignments on time, and follow the instructions for each assignment completely and correctly. If you do not achieve all three goals, you will not be promoted [12].

6   "There is one more thing. The owner of the Pet Emporium called me and said he wants an assistant to help feed and take care of the pets after school, three days a week, for two hours each day. I spoke about this idea with your parents, and they said it was okay with them if you want to take the job. They also know that, as "pay," the store owner would give your family a $30 gift certificate each week that can be used to buy food at the supermarket. If you decide to take the job, you would have to work very hard and be very responsible. Think over what I said, and tomorrow I want you to tell me your thoughts and your decision about the job offer."

7   As John walked out of Ms. Campbell's office and started home, he felt scared about what his parents would say when he got home but also grown-up that he would be helping them by working at the pet store. **(I)** <u>He thought about how Ms. Campbell said he is bright but that he had been acting like a loser. He thought she was right. He had been making very bad choices lately. He remembered how important it was last year to do his schoolwork well and get on the honor roll. He remembered how he had hoped his parents would be pleased if he got very good grades and pictured how happy they actually were when he got them</u> [24]. **(J)** <u>John had confidence that if he put forth a lot of effort and stayed focused on his goals, he would be successful</u> [23].

8   John tried to imagine what the next few weeks would be like. **(K)** <u>He pictured straightening out his stuff, keeping his desk neat and organized so he could find what he needed, and starting his work the same time each day</u> [1]. If he was not going to mess up and forget something, he thought, he probably also **(L)** <u>needed to create routines and do the work in the same order each day</u> [13] and be extra careful about paying attention to what the assignment actually said. **(M)** <u>He also tried to imagine that it was the end of June. He pictured Ms. Campbell congratulating him and saying, "I knew you could accomplish so much if you tried," and his parents hugging him and telling him that they were proud of him for helping his family out and showing how bright he was. It was really important to John to make this picture come true</u> [29].

9   When he got home, John's parents were waiting for him. Instead of being angry, they asked him to tell them what he heard Ms. Campbell say in order to be sure that everyone had the same understanding. John started talking, and to his surprise, began to cry. Tearfully, he explained that school seemed to be a waste of time and that each night, instead of doing his homework, he would play on the computer. His parents said, "We are a family, and we will work together to get things back to the way they should be. **(N)** <u>If you want to take this job, you can, but only if you are sure that you can keep up with your schoolwork. We are not going to tell you what to do about the job. After supper, we want to hear your thoughts and help you make a good decision</u>" [18]. They also mentioned that Aunt Jane, his mom's sister who taught at another school, offered to help John if he wants her to.

10   After supper, John told his parents that it was very important to him to take the job at the Pet Emporium, and he felt that he could do the job and also do well at school. John went on to say that to be sure that he did his best, he would accept Aunt Jane's help.

His parents said okay. The next day, at school, John said to Ms. Campbell that he would take the pet store job. He also told her that he would like to again bet her that not only would he pass all his classes, he would be on the very high honor roll by the end of June. Ms. Campbell said that she would be glad to make the bet again and that she would call the owner of the pet store to tell him that John would start work on Monday.

11 That weekend, he met with his Aunt Jane. She helped him make a schedule so that he could keep track of what he had to do. She explained that (O) <u>John might keep track of the assignments that he has to complete and the specific ways that he hopes to act in order to feel as proud of himself as possible and keep comparing these ideal ways of acting with how he actually acts</u> [27]. John thought about what Aunt Jane said and (P) <u>imagined himself as someone who creates specific, very detailed strategies to get his work done and carefully writes down assignments, checks to be sure that the assignments have been done correctly, and remembers to pay attention in class</u> [19]. Aunt Jane asked him to (Q) <u>write the ways he hopes to act on a piece of paper. She explained that people usually keep to a plan better if they use a recording system and check on how they are doing regularly—that is, self-monitor their behavior at specific times each day</u> [2].

12 On Monday, John was able to act the way he had hoped to in school but had trouble concentrating. He couldn't stop thinking about starting his new job right after school. Finally, the school day ended and he went to the pet store. The owner, who introduced himself as Dan, told John that he had a very important job. (R) <u>He told John it was important that he focus on what he needed to accomplish at the pet store to be a good worker, and explained that John had only two jobs: keeping the cages very clean and feeding the pets—making sure each pet got the right food</u> [25]. As his Aunt Jane did, Dan suggested that John make a list of the things that he had to do, and the order that he would do them in, so that he would not make a mistake. As he started cleaning the cages, John (S) <u>felt very responsible for the living things that he would be taking care of. Because being a kind person was so important to John, he wanted to think of ways that he could be very good at caring for the pets. He decided to write on a piece of paper: "Be an extra-careful worker" and look at the saying each hour on the hour and then make sure he had done the things that he was supposed to do</u> [3]. (T) <u>He also planned to do each of his jobs in the same sequence and at the same time each day</u> [4].

13 At school each day, (U) <u>John monitored his progress to see whether he was achieving the goals that the teachers had set, and he regularly compared how he was acting with the way he wanted to act. He felt happy with how he was doing up until Friday</u> [21]. Thursday evening, when his parents thought that he was asleep, he had heard them talking about how worried they were about being able to pay the bills that month. Earlier in the week, before he had overheard his parents' conversation about bills, (V) <u>John had been able to keep his attention focused while doing schoolwork by saying such things to himself as "I need to act like an honor student," "Look</u>

carefully at the directions," and "Did I skip anything?" [26]. **(W)** <u>He also had been able to notice cues in the classroom to remind himself of what he needed to do, and he had especially been good at noting the assignments that the teacher wrote on the top right side of the board</u> [9].

14 On Friday in math class, though, he kept thinking about his parents' words and felt upset. **(X)** <u>John realized pretty quickly that he was not paying attention as he had intended to. He felt happy that he was able to see right away the difference between how he wanted to act and how he was actually acting</u> [6], and **(Y)** <u>he remembered a technique that a teacher had described to help calm down. She had said that he should focus on his breathing and clear his mind. John tried to do just what the teacher had demonstrated—and it worked. He actually felt calmer and could focus</u> [20]. **(Z)** <u>John was able to quickly solve the math problems that the teacher had written on the board. He felt proud of himself. He thought, "I am a very good math student." He also felt proud that he had realized so quickly that he was distracted, and he felt confident that if he needed to calm down in the future, he could do so by using that breathing technique</u> [22].

15 Work that Friday also did not go well. John loved almost everything about the job except one part—poop. He hated to clean up the poop in the cages and would keep putting it off. When Dan noticed that it was getting late and John had not yet cleaned the cages, he reminded John that he had to keep to the order of the tasks on the list. **(AA)** <u>John thought he needed Dan's advice to help him do what he was supposed to do. He carefully thought about what he wanted to ask Dan and the best time to ask for his help. When he saw that Dan was not busy, he approached him and asked whether Dan could suggest a way that John would not put off the unpleasant task that they had discussed</u> [28]. Dan suggested that he do the unpleasant task first and get it over with. From then on, that is what John did.

16 As the days passed, John found that **(BB)** <u>he was again liking school, especially science, and saw that because he was interested in what the teacher was talking about, it was now easy to pay attention</u> [11]. It also seemed easier and easier for John to remember to do the things that he had to do at school, do them correctly, and **(CC)** <u>notice and feel proud of himself when he did something right</u> [14]. Best of all, his dad had been called back to work, and his parents no longer seemed worried about paying the bills.

17 In the last week in June, when the teachers handed in the grades, Ms. Campbell called John into her office. In a teasing way, she asked John to guess whether he thought he won their bet. John said he was not sure but hoped he had. She said, in fact, he had won the bet and that she was very proud of him. She asked John what he thought he had learned from this year. John paused before answering and said, **(DD)** <u>"It is up to me if I am good at school. If I try hard and put forth a lot of effort, I can be successful</u> [32]. **(EE)** <u>I also learned that I can always improve my abilities if I plan carefully, pick good strategies, and work hard</u> [10]. **(FF)** <u>And, I see that I am responsible for how things go—I can either choose to do my best or not. It is up to me"</u> [30].

Key Ideas Associated with Academic Self-Regulation: Answer Key

Academic self-regulation is likely to be improved when . . .

_K_	1.	The student's home environment is organized and predictable.
_Q_	2.	The student uses a recording system as part of self-monitoring—and the system includes specific behaviors to be tracked and states a schedule for when self-monitoring will occur.
_S_	3.	The student thinks about the personal characteristics that he or she values the most when selecting goals and standards
_T_	4.	The student plans which tasks to do, in what order, and when.
_E_	5.	The student sees the schoolwork as useful.
_X_	6.	The student makes note of any differences between his or her intentions and actual behavior.
_D_	7.	The student exerts willpower and self-control while performing schoolwork.
_G_	8.	The student does not put off doing tasks.
_W_	9.	The student selects cues as reminders to carry out his or her strategies.
_EE_	10.	The student views ability as something that can be improved with effort and the right strategy.
_BB_	11.	The student thinks that academic tasks are interesting.
_H_	12.	The student's goals include a clear definition of success and the time when success will be achieved.
_L_	13.	The student establishes and follows a routine.
_CC_	14.	The student focuses on what he or she does right when doing schoolwork.
_F_	15.	The student understands the need to stay focused on information relevant to achieving his or her goals.
_A_	16.	The student considers schoolwork to be important—and is thereby more motivated to apply effort.
_C_	17.	The student sees academic tasks as valuable and leading to future rewards or benefits.
_N_	18.	The student's parents, teachers, and other important adults are not over-controlling and allow collaboration.
_P_	19.	The student creates specific, detailed strategies to achieve goals.
_Y_	20.	The student can calm himself or herself when distressed while doing school-work and can stay focused on what he or she needs to learn.
_U_	21.	The student regularly monitors his or her actual behavior at school and compares it with what he or she wants to do (or feels he or she ought to do).

___Z___ 22. The student is confident in his or her abilities and has a positive image about himself or herself as a student.

___J___ 23. The student expects to be successful.

___I___ 24. The student thinks about what is valuable or important in doing a good job on schoolwork.

___R___ 25. The student can think about the end point of a task—that is, he or she can answer the question "What do I want to accomplish?"

___V___ 26. The student uses private speech to help manage and control his or her attention while doing school tasks.

___O___ 27. The student thinks about a possible "academic self" and compares his or her actions to those of the possible academic self.

___AA___ 28. The student thinks before asking for help and considers whom to ask, when to ask, and what to ask.

___M___ 29. The student regularly visualizes future academic successes and the benefits that will occur as a result.

___FF___ 30. The student is allowed to make choices in regard to schoolwork—and therefore feels more accountable.

___B___ 31. The student is engaged in schoolwork and sees it as relevant to his or her concerns.

___DD___ 32. The student believes that effort is critical to academic success and thinks that a positive outcome is within his or her control.

References

Allport, D. (1989). Visual attention. In M. I. Posner (Ed.), *Foundations of cognitive science* (pp. 631–682). Cambridge, MA: MIT Press.

Altermatt, E. R., & Pomerantz, E. M. (2003). The development of competence-related and motivational beliefs: An investigation of similarity and influence among friends. *Journal of Educational Psychology, 95,* 11–123.

Ashby, F. G., Isen, A. M., & Turken, A. U. (1999). A neuropsychological theory of positive affect and its influence on cognition. *Psychological Review, 106,* 529–550.

Bandura, A. (1977). Self-efficacy: Toward a unifying theory of behavioral change. *Psychological Review, 84,* 191–215.

Bandura, A. (1982). Self-efficacy mechanism in human agency. *American Psychologist, 37,* 122–147.

Bandura, A. (1997). *Self-efficacy: The exercise of control.* New York: Freeman.

Bandura, A. (1999). Exercise of agency in personal and social change. In E. Sanavio (Ed.), *Behavior and cognitive therapy today: Essays in honor of Hans J. Eyesenck* (pp. 1–29). Oxford, England: Anonima Romana.

Bandura, A., & Cervone, D. (1983). Self-evaluative and self-efficacy mechanisms governing the motivational effects of goal systems. *Journal of Personality and Social Psychology, 45,* 1017–1028.

Battle, E. S. (1965). Motivational determinants of academic task persistence. *Journal of Personality and Social Psychology, 2,* 209–218.

Battle, A., & Wigfield, A. (2003). College women's value orientations toward family, career, and graduate school. *Journal of Vocational Behavior, 62,* 56–75.

Baumeister, R. F., Heatherton, T. F., & Tice, D. M. (1994). *Losing control: How and why people fail at self-regulation.* New York: Academic Press.

Baumrind, D. (1971). Current patterns of parental authority. *Developmental Psychology Monographs, 4,* 1–103.

Bieling, P. J., Isreali, A., Smith, J., & Antony, M. M. (2003). Making the grade: The behavioural consequences of perfectionism in the classroom. *Personality and Individual Differences, 35,* 163–178.

Blair, C. (2002). School readiness: Integrating cognition and emotion in a neurobiological conceptualization of children's functioning at school entry. *American Psychologist, 57,* 111–127.

Bouffard-Bouchard, T. (1990). Influence of self-efficacy on performance in a cognitive task. *Journal of School Psychology, 130,* 353–363.

Bowlby, J. (1979). *The making and breaking of affectional bonds.* London: Tavistock.

Brand, S., Reimer, T., & Opwis, K. (2007). How do we learn in a negative mood? Effects of a negative mood on transfer and learning. *Learning and Instruction, 17,* 1–16.

Brier, N. (2006). *Enhancing academic motivation: An intervention program for young adolescents.* Champaign, IL: Research Press.

Brier, N. (2007). *Motivating children and adolescents for academic success: A parent involvement program.* Champaign, IL: Research Press.

Buhs, E. S., Ladd, G. W., & Herald, S. L. (2006). Peer exclusion and victimization: Processes that mediate the relation between peer group rejection and children's classroom engagement and achievement. *Journal of Educational Psychology, 98,* 1–13.

Butler, R. (1998). Age trends in the case of social and temporal comparison for self-evaluation: Examination of a novel developmental hypothesis. *Child Development, 69,* 1054–1073.

Campos, J. J., Frankel, C. B., & Camras, L. (2004). On the nature of emotional regulation. *Child Development, 75,* 377–394.

Carver, C. S., & Scheier, M. F. (1982). Control theory: A useful conceptual framework for personality-social, clinical, and health psychology. *Psychological Bulletin, 92,* 111–135.

Chapman, M., Skinner, E. A., & Baltes, P. B. (1990). Interpreting correlations between children's perceived control and cognitive performance: Control, agency, or means-ends beliefs? *Developmental Psychology, 26,* 246–253.

Cleary, T., & Zimmerman, B. (2002). Self-regulation empowerment program: A school-based program to enhance self-regulation and self-motivated cycles of student learning. *Psychology in the Schools, 4,* 537–550.

Cole, D. A. (1991). Preliminary support for a competence-based model of depression in children. *Journal of Abnormal Psychology, 100,* 181–190.

Connell, J. P., & Wellborn, J. G. (1991). Competence, autonomy, relatedness: A motivational analysis of self system processes. In M. R. Gunnar & L. A. Sroufe (Eds.), *Self processes and development: The Minnesota Symposia on Child Psychology, Vol. 23* (pp. 43–77). Mahwah, NJ: Erlbaum.

Cooley, C. (1902). *Human nature and the social order.* New York: Scribner.

Corno, L. (1989). Self-regulated learning: A volitional analysis. In B. Zimmerman & D. Shunk (Eds.), *Self-regulated learning and academic achievement* (pp. 111–142).

Corno, L. (1993). The best-laid plans: Modern conception of volition and educational research. *Educational Psychology Review, 22,* 14–22. Mawah, NJ: Erlbaum.

Costa, P. T., & McCrae, R. R. (1992). *Revised NEO Personality Inventory (NEO-PI-R) and NEO Five Factor Inventory (NEO-FFI).* Odessa, FL: Psychological Assessment Resources.

Covington, M. V. (1992). *Making the grade: A self-worth perspective on motivation and school reform.* Oxford, England: Cambridge University Press.

Covington, M., & Beery, R. (1976). *Self-worth and school learning.* New York: Holt, Rinehart and Winston.

Csikszentmihalyi, M. (1988). The flow experience and its significance for human psychology. In Csikszentmihalyi, M., & Csikszentmihalyi, I. S. (Eds.), *Optimal experience: Psychological studies of flow in consciousness* (pp. 15–35). Cambridge, MA: Cambridge University Press.

Deci, E. L., & Ryan, R. M. (1985). *Intrinsic motivation and self-determination in human behavior.* New York: Plenum Press.

Deci, E. L., & Ryan, R. M. (2000). The "what" and "why" of goal pursuits: Human needs and the self-determination of behavior. *Psychological Inquiry, 11,* 227–268.

Deci, E. L., Ryan, R. M., & Williams, G. L. (1996). Need satisfaction and the self-regulation of learning. *Learning and Individual Differences, 8,* 165–183.

Derryberry, D., & Reed, M. A. (2002). Anxiety-related attentional biases and their regulation by attentional control. *Journal of Abnormal Psychology, 111,* 225–236.

Dix, T. (1991). The affective organization of parenting: Adaptive and maladaptive processes. *Psychological Bulletin, 110,* 3–25.

Dweck, C. S. (1986). Motivational processes affecting learning. *American Psychologist, 41,* 1040–1048.

Dweck, C. S., & Master, A. (2008). Self theories motivate self-regulated learning. In D. D. Schunk & B. J. Zimmerman (Eds.), *Motivation and self-regulated learning: Theory, research, and applications* (pp. 31–54). Mahwah, NJ: Erlbaum.

Dweck, C. S., & Repucci, N. D. (1973). Learned helplessness and reinforcement responsibility in children. *Journal of Personality and Social Psychology, 25,* 109–116.

Eccles, J., & Parsons, J. (1983). Expectancies, values, and academic behaviors. In J. T. Spence (Ed.), *Achievement and achievement motives: Psychological and sociological approaches* (pp. 75–146). San Francisco: W. H. Freeman.

Eccles, J. S., & Wigfield, A. (1995). In the mind of the achiever: The structure of adolescents' achievement task values and expectancy-related beliefs. *Personality and Social Psychology Bulletin, 21,* 212–225.

Eccles, J. S., Wigfield, A., & Schiefele, V. (2002). Motivation to succeed. In W. Damon & N. Eisenberg (Eds.), *Handbook of child psychology, Vol. 3: Social, emotional, and personality development* (5th ed., pp. 1017–1095). Hoboken, NJ: Wiley.

Eisenberg, N., Thompson Gershoff, E., Fabes, R. A., Shepard, S. A., Cumberland, A. J., Losoya, S. H., Guthrie, I. K., and Murphy, B. C. (2001). Mothers' emotional expressivity and children's behavior problems and social competence: Mediation through children's regulation. *Developmental Psychology, 37,* 475–490.

Elliot, A. J., & Harackiewicz, J. M. (1996). Approach and achievement goals and intrinsic motivation: A mediational analysis. *Journal of Personality and Social Psychology, 70,* 461–475.

Elliot, A. J., & Thrash, T. M. (2004). The intergenerational transmission of fear of failure. *Personality and Social Psychology Bulletin, 30,* 957–971.

Farrer, C., & Skinner, E. (2003). Sense of relatedness as a factor in children's academic engagement and performance. *Journal of Educational Psychology, 95,* 148–162.

Feather, N. T. (1982). *Expectations and actions: Expectancy value models in psychology.* Hillsdale, NJ: Erlbaum.

Feather, N. T. (1988). Values, valences, and course enrollment: Testing the role of personal values within an expectancy value framework. *Journal of Educational Psychology, 80,* 381–391.

Flook, L., Repetti, R. L., & Ullman, J. B. (2005). Classroom social experiences as predictors of academic performance. *Developmental Psychology, 41,* 319–327.

Försterling, F. (1985). Attributional retraining: A review. *Psychological Bulletin, 98,* 495–512.

Fryer, J. W., & Elliot, A. J. (2008). Self-regulation of achievement goal pursuit. In D. H. Schunk & B. J. Zimmerman (Eds.), *Motivation and self-regulated learning: Theory, research, and applications* (pp. 53–75). Mahwah, NJ: Erlbaum.

Gendolla, G., & Brinkman, T. C. (2005). The role of mood states in self-regulation: Effects on action preferences and resource mobilization. *European Psychologist, 10,* 187–198.

Gest, S. D., Rulison, K. L., Davidson, A. J., & Welsh, J. A. (2008). A reputation for success (or failure): The association of peer academic reputations with academic self-concept, effort, and performance across the elementary grades. *Developmental Psychology, 44,* 625–636.

Gollwitzer, P. M. (1999). Implementation intentions: Strong effects of simple plans. *American Psychologist, 54,* 499–503.

Gonzales DeHass, A., Willems, P., & Doan Holbein, M. (2005). Examining the relationship between parental involvement and student motivation. *Educational Psychology Review, 17,* 99–123.

Graham, S., & Barker, G. P. (1990). The down side of help: An attributional-development analysis of helping behavior as a low-ability cue. *Journal of Educational Psychology, 82,* 7–14.

Grolnick, W. S., Ryan, R. M., & Deci, E. L. (1991). Inner resources for school achievement: Motivational mediators for children's perceptions of their parents. *Journal of Educational Psychology, 83,* 508–517.

Hagan, A. S., & Weinstein, C. E. (1995). Achievement goals, self-regulated learning, and the role of classroom context. In P. R. Pintrich (Ed.), *Understanding self-regulated learning* (pp. 43–56). San Francisco: Jossey-Bass.

Harackiewicz, J. (1979). The effects of reward contingency and performance feedback on intrinsic motivation. *Journal of Personality and Social Psychology, 37,* 1352–1363.

Harter, S. (1992). The relationship between perceived competence, affect, and motivational orientation with the classroom: Processes and patterns of change. In A. K. Boggiano & T. S. Pittman (Eds.), *Achievement and motivation: A social-developmental perspective* (pp. 77–113). New York: Cambridge University Press.

Hidi, S., & Ainley, H. (2002). Interest and adolescence. In F. Pagares & T. Urdan (Eds.), *Academic motivation of adolescents* (pp. 247–275). Greenwich, CT: Information Age.

Hidi, S., & Ainley, H. (2008). Interest and self-regulation: Relationships between two variables that influence learning. In D. H. Schunk & B. J. Zimmerman (Eds.), *Motivation and self-regulation: Theory, research, and applications.* New York: Erlbaum.

Hidi, S., & Harackiewiz, J. (2000). Motivating the academically unmotivated: A critical issue for the 21st century. *Review of Educational Research, 70,* 151–179.

Higgins, E. T. (1987). Self-discrepancy: A theory relating self and affect. *Psychological Review, 94,* 319–340.

Higgins, E. T. (1991). Development of self-regulatory and self-evaluative processes: Costs, benefits, and trade-offs. In M. R. Gunnar & L. A. Sroufe (Eds.), *Self-processes and development: The Minnesota Symposia on Child Psychology, Vol. 23* (pp. 126–166). Mahwah, NJ: Erlbaum.

Higgins, E. T. (1997). Beyond pleasure and pain. American Psychologist, *52,* 1280–1300.

Hoeksma, J. B., Oosterlaan, J., & Schipper, E. M. (2004). Emotion regulation and the dynamics of feelings: A conceptual and methodological framework. *Child Development, 75,* 354–360.

Howell, A. J., Watson, D. C., Powell, R. A., & Buro, K. (2006). Academic procrastination: The pattern and correlates of behavioral postponement. *Personality and Individual Differences, 35,* 163–178.

Jacobs, J. E., Langa, S., Osgood, D. W., Eccles, J. S., & Wigfield, A. (2002). Changes in children's self-competence and values: Gender and domain differences across grades one through twelve. *Child Development, 73,* 509–527.

Janis, I. L., & Mann, L. (1977). *Decision making: A psychological analysis of conflict, choice, and commitment.* London: Cassel and Collier Macmillan.

Jones, L. B., Rothbart, M. K., & Posner, M. I. (2003). Development of executive attention in reschool children. *Developmental Science, 6,* 498–504.

Kinderman, T. (1993). Natural peer groups as contexts for individual development: The case of children's motivation in school. *Developmental Psychology, 29,* 970–977.

Knee, C. R., & Zuckerman, M. (1998). A nondefensive personality: Autonomy and control as moderators of defensive coping and self-handicapping. *Journal of Research in Personality, 32,* 115–130.

Kochanska, G., Tjebkes, T. L., & Forman, D. R. (1998). Children's emerging self-regulation of conduct: Restraint, compliance and internalization from infancy to second year. *Child Development, 69,* 1378–1389.

Kuhn, D. C. (1999). Metacognitive development. In L. Balter & C. Tamis-LeMonda (Eds.), *Child psychology: A handbook of contemporary issues* (pp. 259–286). New York: Psychology Press.

Ladd, G. W., Kochenderfer, B., & Coleman, C. C. (1997). Classroom peer acceptance, friendship, and victimization: Distinct relation systems that contribute uniquely to children's school adjustment? *Child Development, 68,* 1181–1197.

Lewis, M. (1992). *Shame: The exposed self.* New York: Free Press.

Linnenbrook, E. A., & Pintrich, P. R. (2002). Motivation as an enabler of academic success. *School Psychology Review, 31,* 313–327.

Logan, G. D. (1988). Toward an instance theory of automatization. *Psychological Review, 95,* 492–527.

Markus, H., & Nurius, P. (1986). Possible selves. *American Psychologist, 41,* 954–969.

Markus, H., & Wurf, E. (1987). The dynamic self-concept: A social psychological perspective. In M. R. Rosensweig & L. M. Porter (Eds.), *Annual review of psychology, Vol. 38* (pp. 299–337). Palo Alto, CA: Annual Reviews.

Marsh, H. (1992). Content specificity between academic achievement and academic self-concept. *Journal of Educational Psychology, 84,* 35–42.

Marsh, H. W., Byrne, B. M., & Shavelson, R. T. (1988). A multifaceted academic self-concept: Its hierarchical structure and its relation to academic achievement. *Journal of Educational Psychology, 80,* 366–380.

Marsh, H., & Seeshing, A. (1997). Causal effects of academic self-concept on academic achievement: Structural equation of longitudinal data. *Journal of Educational Psychology, 89,* 41–54.

Marsh, H., Trautwein, V., Ludtke, O., Koller, O., & Baumert, J. (2005). Academic self-concept, interest, grades, and standardized test scores: Reciprocal effects modes of causal ordering. *Child Development, 76,* 307–416.

McInerney, D. M. (2004). A discussion of future time perspective: Contemporary research. *Educational Psychology Review, 16,* 141–151.

Meichenbaum, D. (1977). *Cognitive behavior modification: An integrative approach.* New York: Plenum Press.

Miller, R. B., & Brickman, S. J. (2004). A model of future-oriented motivation and self-regulation. *Educational Psychology Review, 16,* 9–33.

Mitchell, M. (1993). Situational interest: Its multifaceted structure in the secondary school mathematics classroom. *Journal of Educational Psychology, 85,* 424–436.

Newman, R. S. (1990). Children's help-seeking in the classroom: The role of motivational factors and attitudes. *Journal of Educational Psychology, 82,* 71–80.

Newman, R. S. (2008). The motivational role of adaptive help seeking in self-evaluated learning. In D. H. Schunk & B. J. Zimmerman (Eds.), *Motivation and self-regulated learning: Theory, research, and applications* (pp. 315–337). Mahwah, NJ: Erlbaum.

Nicholls, J. G. (1990). What is ability and why are we mindful of it? A developmental perspective. In R. J. Steinberg & J. Kolligan (Eds.), *Competence considered* (pp. 11–40). New Haven, CT: Yale University Press.

Nicholls, J. G., Cheung, P., Lauer, J., & Patashnick, M. (1989). Individual differences in academic motivation: Perceiving ability, goals, beliefs, and values. *Individual Differences, 1,* 63–89.

Nolen-Hoeksema, S., Girgus, J. S., & Seligman, M. E. P. (1986). Learned helplessness in children: A longitudinal study of depression, achievement and explanatory style. *Journal of Personality and Social Psychology, 51,* 435–442.

Nurmi, J. (1991). How do adolescents see their future? A review of the development of future orientation and planning. *Developmental Review, 11,* 1–59.

Ommundsen, Y., Haugen, R., & Lund, T. (2005). Academic self-concept, implicit theories of ability, and self-regulation strategies. *Scandinavian Journal of Educational Research, 49,* 461–474.

Oyserman, D., Bybee, D., Terry, K., & Hart-Johnson, T. (2004). Possible selves as road maps. *Journal of Research in Personality, 38,* 130–148.

Oyserman, D., & Terry, K. (2006). Possible selves and academic outcomes: How and when possible selves impel action. *Journal of Personality and Social Psychology, 91,* 188–204.

Paris, S. G., & Byrnes, J. P. (1989). The instructionist approach to self-regulation and learning in the classroom. In B. J. Zimmerman & D. H. Schunk (Eds.), *Self-regulated learning and academic achievement: Theory, research, and practice* (pp. 168–200). New York: Springer-Verlag.

Paris, S. G., Byrnes, J. P., & Paris, A. H. (2001). Constructing theories, identities, and actions of self-regulated learners. In B. J. Zimmerman & D. H. Schunk (Eds.), *Self-regulated learning and academic achievement: Theoretical perspectives* (2nd ed., pp. 253–287). Mahwah, NJ: Erlbaum.

Perry, N. E. (1998). Young children's self-regulated learning and contexts that support it. *Journal of Educational Psychology, 90,* 715–729.

Pham, L. B., & Taylor, S. E. (1999). From thought to action: Effects of process- versus outcome-based mental simulations of performance. *Personality and Social Psychology Bulletin, 25,* 250–260.

Pintrich, P. R., & DeGroot, E. V. (1990). Motivational and self-regulated learning components of classroom academic performance. *Journal of Educational Psychology, 82,* 33–40.

Pomerantz, E. M., Wang, G., & Ng, F. F. (2005). Mother's affect in the homework context: The importance of staying positive. *Developmental Psychology, 41,* 414–427.

Posner, M. I., & Petersen, S. E. (1990). The attention system of the human brain. *Annual Review of Neuroscience, 13,* 24–42.

Pressley, M. T., & Woloshyn, V. (Ed.). (1995). *Cognitive strategy instruction that really improves children's academic performance* (2nd ed.). Brookline, MA: Cambridge University Press.

Prochaska, J. O. (1979). *Systems of psychotherapy: A transtheoretical analysis.* Homewood, IL: Dorsey.

Prochaska, J.O., Redding, C., & Evers, K. (2002). *The transtheoretical model and stages of change.* In K. Glanz, F. M. Lewis, & B. K. Rimer (Eds.), *Health behavior and health education: Theory, research, and practice* (3rd ed.). San Francisco: Jossey-Bass.

Reid, R. (1996). Research in self-monitoring with students with learning disabilities: The present, the prospects, the pitfalls. *Journal of Learning Disabilities, 29,* 314–330.

Roeser, R. W., Eccles, J. S., & Someroff, A. J. (1998). Academic and emotional functioning in early adolescents: Longitudinal relations, patterns, and prediction by experience in middle school. *Development and Psychopathology, 10,* 321–352.

Rokeach, M. (1973). *The nature of human values.* New York: Free Press.

Rothbart, M. K., & Jones, L. B. (1998). Temperament, self-regulation, and education. *School Psychology Review, 27,* 479–491.

Ruff, H. A., & Rothbart, M. K. (1996). *Attention in early development: Themes and variations.* New York: Oxford University Press.

Ryan, A. (2001). The peer group as a context for the development of young adolescent motivation and achievement. *Child Development, 72,* 1135–1150.

Sansone, C., & Thomas, D. B. (2005). Interest as the missing motivator in self-regulation. *European Psychologist, 10,* 175–186.

Sansone, C., Wiebe, D. J., & Morgan, C. (1999). Self-regulating interest: The moderating role of hardiness and conscientiousness. *Journal of Personality, 67,* 701–733.

Sarason, I. G. (1972). Experimental approaches to test anxiety: Attention and the uses of information. In C. D. Sprelberger (Ed.), *Anxiety: Current trends in theory and research, Vol. 2* (pp. 381–403). New York: Academic Press.

Schiefele, V., Krapp, A., & Winteler, A. (1992). Interest as a predictor of academic achievement: A meta-analysis of research. In K. A. Rennenger, S. Hidi, & A. Krapp (Eds.), *The role of interest in learning and development* (pp. 183–212). Mahwah, NJ: Erlbaum.

Schraw, G., Wadkins, T., & Olafson, L. (2007). Doing the things we do: A grounded theory of academic procrastination. *Journal of Educational Psychology, 99,* 12–25.

Schunk, D. H. (1996). Goal and self-evaluative influences during children's cognitive skill learning. *American Educational Research Journal, 33,* 359–382.

Schunk, D. H., & Pajares, F. (2002). The development of academic self-efficacy. In A. Wigfield & J. Eccles (Eds.), *Development of achievement motivation* (pp. 16–31). San Diego: Academic Press.

Schwartz, D., Gorman, A. H., Nakavicoto, J., & Toblin, R. (2005). Victimization in the peer group and children's academic functioning. *Journal of Educational Psychology, 97,* 425–435.

Seligman, M. E. P. (1975). *Helplessness: On depression, development, and death.* San Francisco: Freeman.

Shafran, R., & Mansell, W. (2001). Perfectionism and psychopathology: A review of research and treatment. *Clinical Psychology Review, 21,* 879–906.

Shapiro, E. S., & Cole, L. L. (1999). Self-monitoring in assessing children's problems. *Psychological Assessment, 11,* 448–457.

Sideridis, G. D. (2005). Goal orientation, academic achievement, and depression: Evidence in favor of a revised goal theory framework. *Journal of Educational Psychology, 97,* 366–375.

Simons, J., Vansteenkiste, M., Lens, W., & Lacante, M. (2004). Placing motivation and future time perspective theory in a temporal perspective. *Educational Psychology Review, 16,* 121–138.

Skinner, E. A. (1991). Development and perceived control: A dynamic model of action in context. In M. R. Gunnar & L. A. Sroufe (Eds.), *Self processes and development: The Minnesota Symposia on Child Psychology, Vol 23* (pp. 167–215). Mahwah, NJ: Erlbaum.

Skinner, E. A. (1995). *Perceived control, motivation, and coping.* Thousand Oaks, CA: Sage.

Skinner, E. A., & Belmont, M. J. (1993). Motivation in the classroom: Reciprocal effects of teacher behavior and student engagement across the school year. *Journal of Educational Psychology, 85,* 571–581.

Skinner, E.A., & Edge, K. (2002). Self-determination, coping, and development. In E. L. Deci & R. M. Ryan (Eds.), *Self-determination theory: Extensions and applications* (pp. 297–337). Rochester, NY: University of Rochester Press.

Soenens, B., Elliot, A. J., Goossens, I., Vansteenkiste, M., Luyten, P., & Durciez, B. (2005). The intergenerational transmission of perfectionism: Parents' psychological control as an intervening variable. *Journal of Family Psychology, 19,* 358–366.

Spurr, I. M., & Stopa, L. (2002). Self-focused attention in the treatment of social phobia. *Journal of Abnormal Psychology, 105,* 61–69.

Steel, P. (2007). The nature of procrastination: A meta-analytic and theoretical review of quintessential self-regulatory failure. *Psychological Bulletin, 133,* 65–94.

Steinberg, L., & Silverberg, S. (1986). The vicissitudes of autonomy in early adolescence. *Child Development, 57,* 841–851.

Thomas, C. R., & Gadbois, S. A. (2007). Academic self-handicapping: The role of self-concept clarity and students' learning strategies. *British Journal of Educational Psychology, 77,* 101–119.

Urdan, T., & Midgley, C. (2001). Academic self-handicapping: What we know, what more is there to learn? *Educational Psychology Review, 13,* 115–138.

Vygotsky, L. (1962). *Thought and language.* Cambridge, MA: MIT Press.

Weiner, B. (1986). *An attribution theory of motivation and emotion.* New York: Springer-Verlag.

Wentzel, K. R. (1999). Social-motivational processes and interpersonal relationships: Implications for understanding motivation at school. *Journal of Educational Psychology, 91,* 76–97.

Wentzel, K. R., & Wigfield, A. (1998). Academic and social motivational influences on students' academic performance. *Educational Psychology Review, 10,* 155–175.

Wigfield, A. (1994a). Expectancy-value theory achievement motivation: A developmental perspective. *Educational Psychology Review, 6,* 49–78.

Wigfield, A. (1994b). The role of children's achievement values in the self-regulation of learning outcomes. In D. H. Schunk & B. J. Zimmerman (Eds.), *Self-regulation of learning and performance: Issues and educational applications* (pp 101–124). Mahwah, NJ: Erlbaum.

Wigfield, A., & Eccles, J. S. (1992). The development of achievement task values: A theoretical analysis. *Developmental Review, 19,* 265–310.

Wigfield, A., Eccles, J. S., Yoon, K. S., Harold, R. D., Arbreton, A., Freedman-Doan, C. et al. (1997). Changes in children's competency beliefs and and subjective task values across the elementary school years: A three-year study. *Journal of Educational Psychology, 89,* 451–469.

Winne, P. H. (1997). Experimenting to bootstrap self-regulated learning. *Journal of Educational Psychology, 89,* 397–410.

Wolfe, B. E. (2003). Knowing the self: Building a bridge from basic research to clinical practice. *Journal of Psychotherapy Integration, 13,* 83–95.

Wolters, C. A. (2003). Understanding procrastination from a self-regulated learning perspective. *Journal of Educational Psychology, 95,* 179–187.

Wolters, C. A., & Rosenthal, H. (2000). The relation between students' motivational beliefs and their use of motivational regulation strategies. *International Journal of Educational Research, 33,* 801–820.

Wood, D., Bruner, J., & Ross, G. (1976). The role of tutoring in problem-solving. *Child Psychology and Psychiatry, 17,* 89–100.

Zelazo, P. D., Carter, A., Reznick, J. S., & Frye, D. (1997). Early development of executive function: A problem-solving framework. *Review of General Psychology, 1,* 198–226.

Zimbardo, P. G., & Boyd, J. N. (1999). Putting time in perspective: A valid, reliable individual difference metric. *Journal of Personality and Social Psychology, 77,* 1271–1288.

Zimmerman, B. J. (1989a). A social cognitive view of self-regulated, academic learning. *Journal of Educational Psychology, 81,* 329–339.

Zimmerman, B. J. (1989b). Self-regulated learning and academic achievement. In B. Zimmerman & D. H. Schunk (Eds.), *Self-regulated learning and academic achievement: Theory, research and practice* (pp. 1–25). New York: Springer-Verlag.

Zimmerman, B. J. (2008). Goal setting: A key proactive source of academic self-regulation. In D. H. Schunk & B. J. Zimmerman (Eds.), *Motivation and self-regulated learning: Theory, research, and applications* (pp. 267–295). Mahwah, NJ: Erlbaum.

Zimmerman, B. J., & Bandura, A. (1994). Impact of self-regulatory influences on writing course attainment. *American Educational Research Journal, 31,* 845–862.

Zimmerman, B. J., Bandura, A., & Martinez-Pons, M. (1992). Self-motivation for academic attainment: The role of self-efficacy beliefs and personal goal setting. *American Educational Research Journal, 29,* 663–676.

Zimmerman, B. J., & Schunk, D. H. (2008). Motivation: An essential dimension of learning. In D.H. Schunk & B. J. Zimmerman (Eds.), *Motivation and self-regulated learning: Theory, research, and application* (pp. 1–30). Mahwah, NJ: Erlbaum.

About the Author

Dr. Norman Brier received his doctoral degree in psychology from Yeshiva University. Currently, he is professor of pediatrics and psychiatry at Albert Einstein College of Medicine, Bronx, New York, where he directs an adolescent division focusing on youngsters with histories of chronic school failure. He is the author of *Enhancing Academic Motivation: An Intervention Program for Young Adolescents* and *Motivating Children* and *Adolescents for Academic Success: A Parent Involvement Program,* also published by Research Press, as well as many articles and chapters addressing the psychological and social difficulties of adolescents with learning and developmental disabilities. In addition, he maintains a private practice in Westchester County, New York.